Brenda Hurd
and
Miracle Hurd

Candy Crush Mania
How The Game of Candy Crush Changed Our Lives Forever

Copyright © 2015 Brenda Hurd and Miracle Hurd
All rights reserved.
ISBN-13: 978-1-943093-44-1

Australia – Barbados – China – India – Japan – New Zealand
South Africa – United Kingdom – United States

Published in the United Kingdom by
Dignity Publishing
For information about publishing with Dignity Publishing
please contact us at www.dignitypublishing.com

"We made a mother and child journey and discovered a gem so beautiful we decided to share it with our readers."

Brenda Hurd & Miracle Hurd

Table of Contents

Dedication vi

Acknowledgements vii

Preface x

Introduction xiv

Chapter 1: Life In Our Household 1

Chapter 2: What Is Candy Crush Saga? 6

Chapter 3: Does Cady Crush Have Magical Powers? 23

Chapter 4: Playing With My Younger Brother 34

Chapter 5: Mummy Joins The Game 38

Chapter 6: Candy Crush Follows Me Everywhere 43

Chapter 7: Battle Over The Cookie 48

Chapter 8: We Are Candy Crush Lovers 51

Chapter 9: Candy Crush Summer Holidays 54

Chapter 10: Candy Crush Ambassadors 66

Chapter 11: Family Bonding Through Candy Crush 71

Chapter 12: Candy Crush Diaries: Varying Opinions 84

Chapter 13: Candy Crush, Celebrities and the Media 92

Chapter 14: Candy Crush: The Good, the Bad and the Ugly 95

Chapter 15: Look To The Future 103

About The Authors 109

Bibliography 111

Dedication

To Master Excellence Hurd, the star of *Candy Crush Mania* who cried more tears than any other Candy Crush player in the world we know.

To the daddy of the house, Gordon Hurd who was the greatest arbiter during our Candy Crush fights.

To all Candy Crush lovers out there, keep crushing those candies!

Acknowledgements

To God, Almighty for giving us the gift of a family to share such experiences with.

To my meticulous and loving husband and father to our children Gordon, who went through this book line by line in his usual meticulous and fastidious way, edited, formatted, designed and published it with the help of the formidable team at his company Dignity Publishing. What a husband!

To my Dad and Mum Henry and Grace Gwanvoma who deprived themselves of all comfort to give me an excellent education. Without that sacrifice I would not be able to hold a pen, let alone write. *Nfa Njika Njamu*. Thank you very much.

To my Mother-in-law Nah Mary Fondo who endured cutbacks as we raced to get this project off the ground.

To my first daughter Miracle who took the challenge and helped write several chapters of this book while attending school during the day and writing in the evenings and weekends instead of playing. Baby I am so proud of you.

To Ulrich, Sylvine, Kaleb and Kayla Lamb for the fantastic summer holiday visit featured in this book.

To my sister-in-law, Blossom who, though absent for academic and family reasons, was a force behind the realisation of this book.

Candy Crush Mania

To everyone at King Digital Entertainment, the creators of Candy Crush Saga, who invented this phenomenal online game.

To all Candy Crush lovers, players and enthusiasts who form the worldwide Candy Crush Kingdom.

To all parents who are wondering what in God's Name is Candy Crush and why their children play it non-stop.

To Carlos, Adelaide, Maeva, and Lea Cequeira for being enthusiastic Candy Crush players and lovers and for always giving us free lives on Facebook. You guys rock!

To Charlie Koumakou who joined us to play the game as I made this journey.

To Shamiso, her husband Tomy and her perspicacious daughter Yasmine for being such great Candy Crush companions.

To Miracle's English teacher, Miss Matthews for being the best teacher a student could ever have and for pushing her further each time. If everyone had a teacher like you, I think we'd all be authors!

To Miracle's best friends Zainab, twins David & Lewis, Harry, Mercaides-Paris, Lauren, Lewis, Amber, Sasha, Moyo, Antonia, Wanessa, Monica, Shaniece, Tadi, Sophie, Rosie, Olivia, Abbie Leigh, Jessica, Mollie, Millie, Kerry, Emma, Nyrisha, Teannah, Josie, Josey, Joanne 'Laura' and Nancy. You've all inspired me and I love you all. Thank you for being the best friends you can be

Acknowledgements

in different ways. You are such a great inspiration. Always be you and follow your dreams!

I acknowledge all children who have been placed in my care in the past including Gretchen, Maya and Zara Mbuyongha, Esther, Dare and Joseph Ilesanmi, Moyo and Damilade Odubanjo. You helped build memories that form parts of this book.

To the creators of Facebook, Mark Zuckerberg with his college roommates and fellow Harvard University students Eduardo Saverin, Andrew McCollum, Dustin Moskovitz and Chris Hughes who created a revolution in human social life.

To our book cover designers Carisa, Nehara and Max who endured dozens of revisions as we worked to produce the perfect cover. Thank you all very much.

Our sincere gratitude goes to Willy Nkono for travelling all the way to take great pictures for this project. Merci Willy.

We cannot leave out our web designer Rashidul Islam who, as we write, is working relentlessly to polish our website.

To any and everyone we may have left out, we apologize. Your contribution is much appreciated.

Brenda Hurd and Miracle Hurd

Preface

When my wife Brenda and daughter Miracle interrupted my movie time in our living room to "pledge allegiance that we will write a book on Candy Crush within the next 30 days", I consulted my calendar fearing it was a sick April fool's joke. It was not.

At first I scoffed at the idea and wondered why of all themes in the world they would choose to write a book about a game of candies. As I mauled over the idea for a few minutes while they stood waiting, I had a light bulb moment. This was indeed a great idea for a book!

As a personal development expert, life coach and motivational speaker, one of the key aspects of my work is to identify and develop talent in keeping with people's goals. Most of the time I focus on mind over matter as the easiest way to get something done is to hand it over to the subconscious mind. The subconscious mind functions at its best when the conscious mind is pleasurably occupied. One of the ways to occupy the conscious mind and allow the subconscious to do its subterranean work is to play games, participate in or watch sports, watch a movie, read a book, hold pleasant conversations, play with kids or a spouse, or do anything that is pleasant and engaging.

It was on the basis of this that I agreed to throw my weight and resources behind *Candy Crush Mania*. There were of course other considerations. With Candy Crush being played by over 100

Preface

million fans a day, I saw a great opportunity for the authors to engage and share their experience with a community that spans the entire globe.

Candy Crush Mania is born of the daily experiences of my family playing the beautiful game. Prior to Candy Crush, I had been introduced to other rather tough games by my son Excellence and YouTube fans such as *Game of Thrones, Assassin's Creed, Battlefield, Batman, Halo5* and *Minecraft*. It was therefore with great interest that I saw my wife Brenda, a hard-nosed academic, take to Candy Crush with gusto, hard on the heels of my children Miracle, co-author of this book, and her baby brother Excellence. At first I thought it was a transient experience but as the days went by, I noticed I had to plead with her every night to please dim the lights so I could sleep, so glued was she to the game! Sometimes in between bouts of sleep, I would hear her and my daughter Miracle giggling like two school girls on their first prom night as they exploded candies! What a nightmare!

One of the pathways to success is to turn your passion into profit. The great Brian Tracy, motivational speaker extraordinaire, once said that if you find yourself doing something for hours on end, enjoy it thoroughly and can do it without getting paid for it, then that is an indication that you are called to do it. The deep passion of the authors of this book for Candy Crush stands them in good stead to write *Candy Crush Mania*.

I find that gamers often feel guilty about playing as the world describes them as idle or purposeless. This book debunks that myth. See what King Digital Entertainment has done with a game. See what Brenda and Miracle are doing with their love of Candy Crush. The former created a multi-billion dollar company through the game. The latter are publishing a book which will lift them into even greater heights.

Candy Crush Mania is testament to the fact that you can take goodness out of anything, even the things that society scoffs at and derides, such as gaming. You can use a game to engage and bond with your family as we have done. You can write about your experience as Brenda and Miracle have done. You can draw inspiration from the tribulations and trials of the game's creators and apply it to your own personal and business development.

Candy Crush Mania will appeal to lovers of the game worldwide and in these pages they will see their own experiences with the game replicated in book form by two very passionate lovers of the same.

Candy Crush Mania is a great read and I count it a privilege to be associated with such a great work.

Gordon Hurd
Author, Life Coach, Motivational Speaker, Preacher, Provocateur
Father, Husband and Teacher. His books include:
Christian Prosperity Secrets, Two-Time Groom. You Are Far Better Than You Think.
YouTube Channel
www.youtube.com/TheBigManTyrone

Preface

Twitter Page

https://twitter.com/BasedTyrone

Website

www.gordonhurd.tv

Introduction

"I feel like a little kid who just walked into a candy store. I think that's something to smile about".

Brandon Boyd

My kids love to play *Candy Crush Saga*, an online computer game which many of you know and maybe already play. As a parent I take a keen interest in the things my children do. In order to be able to share in their fun and be a part of their childhood experiences, I decided to join them in playing Candy Crush.

This story is about the journey we made as a family with the *Candy Crush Saga* game at the centre of our narrative. Please join us on an unforgettable journey and enjoy this story as *Candy Crush Mania* unfolds right under your watchful eyes.

A lot of the time, people feel guilty about enjoying a good game as the work culture of society has made play a thing of idle, unproductive people. We beg to differ in this book. We explode the myth that play is a waste of time and show how engaging in this beautiful game not only helped us relax, but bonded us together and even given me a deep insight into the business acumen that surrounds the whole concept.

To you Candy Crush lovers out there, I would like to say this: you have full control over what you do with the game. You can play when you want and you can stop whenever you choose. Above all, you can use your experience of the game and turn it into positive energy like we have. Like fire, Candy Crush is a good

Introduction

servant and a bad master. You decide how you want it to affect your life.

It is our wish that you will enjoy this book as much as we have enjoyed playing Candy Crush and writing this book for you. We also look forward to having you tell your own Candy Crush story on our website, in various fora and on social media platforms.

Brenda Hurd

Chapter 1: Life In Our Household

"I want to get a vending machine, with fun sized candy bars, and the glass in front is a magnifying glass. You'll be mad, but it will be too late".

Mitch Hedberg

"Welcome to this century" are the words my daughter Miracle said, as I continually bombarded her with questions on this game and that game. I'm from another generation and although I love to work on computers, I could never be found glued to a screen for more than two hours on a stretch, so I was intrigued to find out more about this game that my children seemed to be playing at all hours of the day and night.

Sorry to say I am not that kind of high-tech mom. I didn't get to see a TV screen till I was 8 years old. I owned a mobile phone for the first time when I was in university, so this new generation of high tech children beat my imagination. They know every button on the computer and TV and can figure out an iPhone within one hour of handling one. When my husband Gordon bought an iPad

Candy Crush Mania

for the kids, I wondered to myself why he was wasting his money on a "toy" that would probably be forgotten in a couple of weeks. I was just thinking about the past and the way children these days treat toys. They are excited about it for a few days and if you are lucky a few weeks and if it is a very good toy maybe they will carry on playing with it for 6 months till the next birthday or Christmas. I remember one Christmas when the baby of the house Excellence got a complicated build-it-yourself toy.

The toy car had over 200 pieces which had to be meticulously assembled piece by piece into a car, filling station and garage parking lot. Usually we let Miracle do the assembly with Excellence. Miracle, who is usually very good at assembling such toys, gave up in less than no time. I joined in and tried to help them out but I was none the wiser. Gordon joined the cue and offered his help but after five days of trying to no avail the pieces kept being pushed further and further into the corner of the living room till one day it was ripe for the bin. Thank you Santa Claus anyway.

So to be honest I did not see why the story would be different with the iPad. I thought the kids would, in their usual manner, get excited about the gadget for a while, then after a few weeks the excitement would wane and they would start pestering us for yet another toy. After all I still have a good functioning Nintendo DS in my bedroom drawer which no one misses or ever asks about anymore. It's been lying there for the past 6 years! But I was mistaken this time; the iPad was not just another toy for both of them; it became the most essential tool in their life. In fact for Miracle it was like a second skin. She went everywhere with it and even when doing her chores the iPad would be lying on the kitchen table as she washed dishes and from time to time changed the music or took a swipe at Candy Crush. This was a phenomenon I could not understand.

Initially, Gordon bought just one iPad with the hope that it was a family gadget. The kids could use it to play and we could use it to work on the go as he does a lot of work online. But the first mistake he made was to offer it to Miracle as a gift with the adjunct that she can use it to play with her brother too.

At the beginning, everything was going well and life kind of returned to normal. Miracle was playing all sorts of games, joining multiple social networks on it and occasionally would play with Excellence. At least they no longer quarrelled over TV programs as there was one more gadget to use. But as their interest in the iPad and all it has to offer rose, we began to settle more and more quarrels and iPad fights between them.

As time went on the disagreements over whose turn it was to use the iPad grew in number and intensity. Even though Excellence is the baby of the house he is very tenacious and would fight for his right to have a go.

"Mummy, Mimi is not sharing." Excellence would say.

"Daddy, Mimi won't let me have a go" Excellence's continual whingeing would carry on, not relenting until he got his way

Candy Crush Mania

through crying.

"Mimi, can I have a go?"

"Daddy, Mimi is being mean."

"Mimi, its my turn now."

"Mimi, let your brother have a go", I would say.

"Excy, you just had a turn 30 minutes ago" Mimi would say in hopes of keeping on playing on her own.

"No that was yesterday".

Basically, Excellence has no notion of time frames and for him time is: *now, today* and *yesterday*. To him if he is not playing on the game now he knows that the last time he remembers playing was yesterday. Now as a parent I understand that his little mind is struggling with the concept of time but Miracle does not or chooses not to. To Miracle her little brother is lying even though she has let him have a go. And sometimes too I would be so amused by his mistaken concept of time and you would find Mimi and I giggling and correcting Excy rather than pacifying him.

But Mimi fancied herself as the custodian and keeper of the key to the iPad. You know she was like Saint Peter guarding the precious key to heaven with his own very dear life. We never even got to touch the iPad when they were at home. Our only hope of using it was when they were in school or asleep. They would quarrel all the time and Excellence (Excy) would be the first to

Life In Our Household

start crying. He would cry and cry and cry till he had his way. Sometimes I would be able to console him and calm him down but for some reason he feels that his complaint is better understood only by his dad.

Excy kind of believes that there are two gangs in the house: a "girls gang" made of Mimi and Mummy and a "boys gang", made of Daddy and himself. And for some reason Gordon too believes that he has to fight for Excy's right especially when he catches us laughing our eyes out during some of Excy's outbursts.

So it does not matter if his dad is asleep, catching up on his work or just relaxing in his study, when Excy is angry he is going straight upstairs to tell his dad. Even if you try to console him once he is in anger mode only his dad can calm him and bring him down from the *"wailing mountain"* as we have come to call it. I cannot count how many times he did this to his dad but one day Gordon was fed up of solving iPad disputes between the kids, so he grabbed his purse went out and bought Excellence his own iPad. He came back and proudly presented the iPad to his son and added "Now no one will bully my son over the iPad".

We thought peace and tranquillity had returned till they discovered the "Candy Crush Saga" game and began to live, eat and sleep in it. Now two ipads have turned to three and Gordon is now considering a fourth ipad to "put paid to this constant gadget war".

But before we delve any further into this book, let us examine the nature of Candy Crush.

Chapter 2: What Is Candy Crush Saga?

"When I was a kid at first I wanted to own a candy shop. I guess every kid wants to - we just want to have access - free access".

Franka Potente

I would like to start this chapter by addressing the use of the word "*Saga*". We all know what candy is and what it means to crush candy but may also have questioned the use of the word *saga*. I remember as I did research on the net regarding what people were saying about the use of the word *saga* in King's games, one man said that King Digital Entertainment had no right to use the word saga. He advised the creators of this game to check their dictionaries before using words incorrectly. I beg to differ here with this guy whose enthusiasm I applaud but whose stance I must gently oppose. According to the Oxford English Dictionary, a saga is a long story of heroic achievement, especially a medieval prose narrative in Old Norse or Old Icelandic. It can also be a long, involved story, account, or series of incidents. I bet anyone who has made it up to level 100 in the game will indeed testify that it's been a veritable saga. With series of incidents involving candy. (http://bit.ly/OxfordAtCandyCrushMania).

In the same light I would suggest that he check his dictionary and he would agree that Candy Crush is indeed a saga. If we look at *Candy Crush Saga*, the first thing we know is that it has a story line. It may not be written but it tells a story. The game may have started with a few episodes but it is indeed a long virtual narrative of many battles through varying types of hostile but sweet terrain. Whether the gamer is in *Candy Town* with its lovely mayor, in the *Chocolate Mountains, Salty Canyon, Jelly Mountains* or *Sticky Savanah* just to name a few, all players would agree that they have to fight veritable excruciating battles to win and move on to the next quest. Synonym's of Saga include: epic, chronicle, legend, folk tale, romance, traditional story, history, narrative, adventure, fairy story, myth; roman-fleuve. If Candy Crush Saga is not an adventure then I wonder what it is. (http://bit.ly/OxfordAtCandyCrushMania

Although many people already know and play Candy Crush, there are still people who do not know what Candy Crush is all about. Some may have only vaguely heard about it and some have never ever played a single episode. The purpose of this chapter is to give some information about the game which will enable people reading this book to better understand the core subject of the narrative. Candy Crush is just one of the games on King's portfolio of enjoyable games.

King has more than 195 fun titles in over 200 countries across the

What Is Candy Crush Saga?

web and on mobile platforms. Their hits include Candy Crush Saga, Farm Heroes Saga, Pet Rescue Saga, Bubble Witch 2 Saga, Diamond Digger Saga and Candy Crush Soda Saga. Their games are synchronized across platforms, allowing players to switch seamlessly between devices and platforms and continue their game wherever they left off, so they can play on any device, anywhere, any time. For all of their Saga format games, players can continue through the game without losing lives as long as they complete each level. Players can also return to specific levels in order to achieve the best "three star rating." (http://company.king.com/our-games/)

Candy Crush Saga is a British-Swedish puzzle game which was released by the game developing company King Digital Entertainment Plc on 12 April 2012. The Chief Executive Officer and co-founder of King Digital Entertainment is Riccardo Zacconi. This online game was first released as a Facebook app in April 2014 and later on in November 2014 as a mobile app for smartphones. Today the game can be played on almost any device: computer, smartphone and tablet.

What Does Candy Crush Look Like?

Optically Candy Crush comprises brightly coloured candy of different shapes. The beauty and splendour alone of these beautifully coloured candies is enough to catch the eye of child and adult alike and make the mouth water even though the candy is virtual. There are different types of candy represented in this game. The first is the very popular jelly bean which is enjoyed by millions worldwide. The jelly bean comes in the colour red and when the player matches four of them the match produces a striped candy. This red and white stripped candy acts as a booster. It can clear a whole row or column of candy on the game board. When a player matches candy in a t-shape, it produces a wrapped candy which is also a booster. When combined during the game up to five rows and five columns of candy are crushed in a swooping manner and the game advances faster. My son Excellence calls this the "Zoom Zang" combination.

Other types of candy found in the game are the orange Lozenges, the yellow lemon drops, the green gum squares, the blue lollipop heads and the purple jujube clusters. All these candy when matched in groups of four produce stripped candy which are boosters. In combination with other striped or packaged candy, these produce special effects and help make the game progress faster.

Another special candy in the game is the blue jelly fish or Swedish fish. When activated they swarm the game and eat up candy, thus bringing the game to a faster win. In our home when the fish appears we all get up and prepare for the victory dance as we know victory is near and you'll hear us all chorusing "fishy fishy fish: red one, blue one, green one, yellow fish, purple fish. Fishy, fishy fish".

Then you have the coconut wheel candy with a liquorice centre. This can either be bought in the yeti shop or on the booster spinning wheel. When switched with a regular candy, it moves in

What Is Candy Crush Saga?

one direction and clears all the candy in its path. Sometimes it appears at the start of a game in higher levels.

There are also other types of Candy like the lucky candy found in higher levels of the game, the extra time candy and the mystery candy with a good or bad outcome when matched with another candy. A chameleon candy is found from level 306 in savoury shores and onwards. It has a pink aura around it and a rainbow that sweeps across the board in a few seconds.

Other special candies which appear on the boards for free can be purchased from the in-game store, or won from the Candy Crush Booster Wheel. These include Jelly Fish in jelly clearing boards which clear 3 pieces from the board at random, the Coconut Wheel on ingredient dropping boards which changes three candies in a row into striped candies, and Lucky Candy in recipe boards which when matched changes to one of the types of pieces the player needs to clear the objective. The Booster Wheel also offers a chance to win a jackpot of all boosters in one spin. Other pieces known as Blockers appear on boards to add to the challenge. Icing (also called Meringues) cannot be moved and can only be removed by matching next to it. Liquorice Locks a cage around single pieces of candy to prevent them from use. Chocolate pieces will multiply if not cleared. Liquorice Swirls cannot be easily removed with Special Candies. Candy Bombs will explode and end the level early if they are not cleared. Multi-layered Icing requires multiple matches to remove. Chocolate Spawners will produce Chocolate pieces at all times. Marmalade guards Special Candies from use. Cake Bombs can clear the entire board once cleared, and Toffee Tornadoes move on the board destroying pieces and shattering the tile beneath them to prevent use for one turn. Other pieces also appear on levels such as Chameleon Candies which switch colours every turn, Mystery Candies which randomly turn into a Special Candy or a Blocker, and Extra Time Candies on time limit levels.

But the star of the game is the "Colour Bomb". Optically it looks like a ball of chocolate with sprinkles on it or Maltesers. When switched with a regular candy, it clears all candy of that colour on the game board. When swiped with a stripped candy, it turns all candy that colour into striped candy which in turn immediately clear each line according to the stripped candy's direction. But the most electrifying moment is when a player has the luck of having two colour bombs together. Man oh Man! The effect is glorious in an explosion of fireworks. It clears all the candy on the game board spraying laser beams in a half moon direction and brings the game to an immediate win almost every time.

Candy Crush Saga is very much like Bejewelled, created by the British Facebook game developing team King.com. The difference between it and Bejewelled is that the game has a story mode; levels can have multiplerequired goals, more entities and elements, and most obviously, has candies instead of jewels. It is currently available through the Apple Store, the Google Play Store, and Facebook for free, with the ability to sync between devices and your Facebook account. There are currently a total of

What Is Candy Crush Saga?

1,480 levels (875 Reality levels and 605 Dreamworld levels). You have to match three or more candies of the same colour through switching candies with each other to complete the various level objectives. There are five types of Levels: Moves Levels, Jelly Levels, Ingredient Drop Levels, Timed Levels, and Candy Order Levels." (http://candy-crush-saga.wikia.com/wiki/World).

There are two worlds in Candy Crush: the real world and the Dream World with an owl called Odus. While playing one has to keep a balance and make sure that Odus does not fall as that would signify an immediate end to the game. This game has gained worldwide popularity and the fact that developers are still working day and night to create new levels for our enjoyment, means that the game has come to stay. A book has a beginning and an end but Candy Crush is an open game, an unfinished pilgrim's journey and its players won't rest till they have conquered the temptations that lie ahead.

Candy Crush operates an in-app store where players can purchase boosters to help them advance in a game and improve their chances of winning. They can also buy lives when they have used the 5 lives apportioned to them at the beginning of each game. Usually players have to wait for their lives to refill, ask their friends on Facebook for lives, or play a mystery quest to unlock next levels. The game is free to download and the choice to buy anything lies with the gamer.

The game is arranged in different episodes. Once levels in a particular episode have been completed, the next episode is locked. The player would now need to unlock further levels. Now to do this the player has three options:

1. Buy from the in-app store

2. Ask friends on Facebook for tickets or

3. Play a mystery quest

Unfortunately on Facebook you cannot do a mystery quest as this is only available on mobile devices.

Three Mystery Quests must be completed before the next episode is unlocked, and a player can only complete one Mystery Quest in a single 24-hour period. Recently the option to unlock episodes by playing mystery quests is only available after several days have passed and no help is received through friend requests on Facebook. Other than waiting the time period until mystery quests are available, using in app purchase is the only way to unlock episodes.

The Brains Behind Candy Crush

The more I played Candy Crush the more I became interested in the lives of the people behind the company. When I hear of great success I try to find out what philosophies those people live by, what makes them tick and what is the secret behind their success.

CEO of King Digital Entertainment: Riccardo Zacconi

As I began my research, I found out that its CEO and co-founder is Riccardo Zacconi. Zacconi was born in 1967 in Rome and

What Is Candy Crush Saga?

studied Economics at the LUIS University of Rome. After his graduation he travelled to London and then to Germany. Ricardo is married and has a three year old son. Zacconi owns 31,042,045 shares in King Digital Entertainment valued at 698 million US dollars.

Prior to founding King, Zacconi, Morris, and Toby Rowland worked together on uDate.com, a site created by Morris. Morris sold the site for $150 million in 2003.[7] The three joined forces with Sebastian Knutsson, Thomas Hartwig, Lars Markgren and Patrik Stymne to found King in 2003.

Udate was later merged with Match.com. Zaccon eventually launched King with colleagues from Spray, and persuaded some of uDate's backers, including Melvyn Morris and Toby Rowland, to join the new venture. Spray missed its window to make it rich after delaying its IPO by a month and was sold to Lycos instead. (http://bit.ly/UdateAtCandyCrushMania).

Many times when we hear success stories we assume that the people just touched one thing and hit the jackpot immediately but this has not been the case with Ricardo. He worked as a consultant for several years before teaming up with some Swedish guys to start a site called Spray in 1999, an online messaging company. A rich family of bankers in ergs invested 100 million dollars in Spray. They missed going on the stock exchange by one month and when NASDAG crashed they had to postpone and finally sold the company in 2000.

Candy Crush Mania

At 46, Zacconi has held a lot of other jobs before his stint as the big cheese at King. Zacconi has a broad range of tech-world experience, which has informed his work at King. According to The Local, Zacconi "has led an international career, including playing marketing cupid for online dating site Match.com and working for Swedish internet company, Spray Network.

One thing I love about Zacconi is the fact that he is not afraid of failure and you can't keep him down for too long. When 'disaster struck' first time he dusted himself up and moved to London where he founded King. The bust was not a disaster for Riccardo but a wakeup call.

Zaccon and his colleagues have built a large collection of games. He argues that by launching so many titles per year they can innovate, because "innovation requires experimentation, and experimentation also implies failure, but we fail fast and cheaply. When we invest considerably more resources with larger teams, we are pretty sure that the game play is good. We have proven the format in which we launch these games also works". (http://bit.ly/GamesAtCandyCrushMania).

There is a certain simplicity about the way Riccardo goes about business that I admire. Whereas some of his competitors are spending millions of dollars and hundreds of staff to develop a game, he has cut it down. According to King, a game should be developed by at most 3 to 5 people and should not last more than 3 months. This keeps costs down. He may fail but he fails forward to success, in the words of Mary Kay Ash, and thus casualties are

What Is Candy Crush Saga?

fewer in number than those of his competitors

Zacconi loves a challenge and is a solution finder. When he was faced with payment gateways he had to find 60 different payment solutions to enable his trade in all countries that were using his services. We take it for granted that everyone has a credit card or uses PayPal but that's not the case. In many countries such as Germany, Italy and Spain few people have credit cards, so he had to find a payment solution adapted to each specific country.

I kind of agree with Riccardo's enthusiasm for tablets. I have played games on almost all possible devices but the best experience is on the swipeable devices as they are small and portable. Not too small like a phone to strain your eyes and not too big like a laptop or desktop to be cumbersome.

Zaconni concurs:

> "I am a super big fan if the iPad mini. It's a fantastic device for gaming. It's more portable than the iPad and allows you to have a much better surfing experience than the iPad. It integrates well and it's a good answer from Apple to their competition. For our game world, it's definitely very positive because from a development effort point of view the games can be immediately played on the iPad. It doesn't need any additional work." (ttp://bit.ly/IpadMiniAtCandyCrushMania).

One would wonder what a man who studied economics at school has to do with games. But he is wise to surround himself with experts in the field. By pitching most of his offices close to universities he is able to capture fresh young talent and invest in people. By listening to his employees they are better able to form a cohesive partnership beneficial to all parties involved. The smartest move Zacconi made was to move with the times. Launching his games on Facebook at the time he did has helped introduce a new gaming era and added to the popularity of the game.

Co Founder and Chairman of King: Melvyn Morris

One of the co-founders of King Digital Entertainment is self-made millionaire and business tycoon Melvyn Morris. He holds the position of Chairman and has done so since the company's creation in 2003. Same as Zacconi, King digital entertainment is not his first business venture.

Morris left school at 16 and by the time he was 20 years old he was already earning a living as a consultant. He travelled to America and worked there for a while before returning to Britain in his home town of Derby. Morris has dipped his hands into a few business pies before finally becoming part of King.

When he returned home from America, he started a few businesses including: a hardwood flooring company, a Spanish property group and a dating agency called uDdate. When uDate was sold in 2002, it was the second-largest dating site in the world. Morris made a net income of £20m after the company was sold. Being the avid and wise business man that he is, he split his profit into two. He spent part of the money buying a stake in his beloved Derby County football club and part of it establishing King.com. I am sure he pats himself every day on the back for making that decision and for believing in this venture even when it

What Is Candy Crush Saga?

came near bankruptcy.

Melvyn Morris owns 36,467,500 shares in King Digital Entertainment and his shareholding is valued at $821 million.

Chief Creative Officer: Sebastian Knutsson

Sebastien Knutsson is the geek in the company. He is the chief creative Officer from whose desk most of the games we play have resurrected. He owns 17,596,075 shares valued at 396 million dollars. Knutsson, the Swedish creative director of gaming company King Digital Entertainment, has been the driving force behind the success of Candy Crush. The game is deceptively simple: a player must match three or more brightly coloured sweets in order to win points and progress to the next level. It's a bit like Tetris, but easier and with fewer hard edges. The sweets seemed like a good idea at the time. Knutsson, 45, says he liked the bold, brash colours of jelly beans, sherbet lemons and barley sugars because they reminded him of the early 1990s arcade games he grew up with.

Candy Crush is a very "simple" game and the basic idea behind it is to match candy according to their colours. The principle behind it is for the player to match three, four or five similar candy to produce an effect or reaction. Each time a player matches three or more candy there is an effect.

Knutsson recently claimed to have designed 10 of the company's 15 worst games – it has made 180 so far – but Candy Crush also emerged from his Stockholm studio. A keen gamer himself, his

vivid designs are inspired by the multi-coloured, flashing and bleeping arcade games of the last century, from Pac-Man to Space Invaders and Tetris.
(http://bit.ly/UdateAtCandyCrushMania).

Knutschen has a Bachelor of Arts degree in Cost-Analysis and Finance from the Stockholm School of Economics. It is often said that a fruit does not fall far from the tree. And this is the case with Knutsson. He comes from a family of entrepreneurs. His parents own a denim brand and a retail chain while his sister owns her own clothing company. He was also a co-founder of Spray where he met Zacconi and a decade later this business relationship has taken them to heights immeasurable.

Chief Technology Officer: Thomas Hartwig

Thomas has been with the other members of the company since their Sray days and has played a pivotal role in the testing phase of the game. He owns 6,350,000 shares in the company with an estimated value of $143 million.

Hartwig is the brains behind King's data strategy; harvesting information from the 1.4bn game plays a day to hone each product from its testing phase on the King.com website through to its launch as a standalone smartphone app.

Thomas is the brain behind the coordination process that takes every game from the time it is launched through its testing phase from King.com to Facebook until it is finally an independent smart phone app. Scientists are placed in groups no bigger than 10.

What Is Candy Crush Saga?

They work together to develop new King games, collate data on user experience and use this information to make decisions on how easy or difficult to make each successive level.

Co-Founder: Toby Rowland

Another co-founder worth mentioning is Toby Rowland who was also Co-chief Executive Officer till 2008. But he prematurely sold his shares in 2011 shy of just a few months before the Facebook version of the game which catapulted the company to a new level. Toby Roland is married to author and Vogue journalist Plum Sykes. He also came from a family of entrepreneurs. his father was the mining tycoon Tiny Rowland, who once owned the Observer and House of Fraser department stores. Morris persuaded him to move to Derby and become marketing director of uDate.

He invested and shared in the spoils when the site was sold for $150m, using the proceeds to set up King. Despite backing the company for eight years, like the founding Beatles member Pete Best, Rowland left too early to share in its success. (http://bit.ly/UdateAtCandyCrushMania).

Toby Rowland had 40m shares in the company. He sold his shares back to the company for a paltry 3m pounds but that is chicken change compared to the 900m dollars which his shareholding is worth as at the time of writing. If he had stayed with King he would be the largest single shareholder with a stake worth 887 million more than what he sold it for.

Candy Crush Mania

Angel investor and former board member Klaus Hommels sold a similar stake at the same time.

The superficial simplicity of Candy Crush belies an extremely sophisticated design process. Riccardo Zacconi, King's CEO and co-founder, has a rule that new games must be built in no more than three months by no more than three people. They are tried out first on King.com. With enough hits, the game will then mutate on to Facebook. If the game proves successful there, only then will it be made available on mobile devices. It is an effective system that keeps costs low.

Zacconi is clearly much more circumspect now that he runs a public company. One thing he is clear on, however is that once the IPO was set in motion, its path was fixed. "It is expensive. It takes time and effort. If you decide to postpone, you have to redo the work... When we decide to do something, we do it", he says.

Other investors and shareholders include: Gerhard Florin, non-executive director whose shares are valued at $25m, Patrick Stymne with shares worth 158m, Stephane Kurgan its chief operating officer with shares of 168m; Lars Markgren who manages the operations in Sweden has 9,043,930 shares worth $203m

Last but not least of its investors is Apax Partners. They are venture capitalists and have invested 3.25 billion US dollars into King.com. Apax holdings across Europe include: the fashion chain New Look, the Orange mobile network, and a trade publishing

What Is Candy Crush Saga?

venture with the Guardians parent company. Apex has a 48% stake in King.com. Its cash injection of 36 million dollars is now worth 100 times that. The mathematics of share multiplication and profit beats my literary brain so I won't even try to figure it out.

As a company, the team of King Digital Entertainment founders and investors do me proud. They are a glaring example of how a partnership should work for the benefit of all parties involved. It shows the value of teamwork and investing in each other. Zacconi alone would not have been able to perform this mammoth task. I do not doubt that they have had hurdles to fight and a few finger waggings in the boardroom but overall their experience makes business partnership worth its while. Some partnerships only lead to bitterness, anger, fighting and acrimony but these guys give a whole new definition to partnership and I doff my hat to them.

Chapter 3: Does Cady Crush Have Magical Powers?

"Sour Patch, Swedish Fish. I love candy, man. I can't go without candy. And when I'm recording, I always have a TV on with cartoons - on mute, though".

Tyga

We cluttered out of the school after Mrs Mathieu handed us our homework sheets. As I turned into the streets with my closest friends, I started counting my steps and stopped to glance back up at my homework.

"Ugh, Jaliyah look at this; Maths homework. Algebra to be precise, I don't like maths at all!" I groaned.

She laughed and smiled. "No one likes Maths really except our one and only Kazeem a.k.a Albert Einstein".

"Trust me, man I've never seen anyone so passionate and good as maths as Kazeem. Sometimes I really do think he knows more than Mrs Mathieu; born a true geek, destined to be forever talented!" I said wonderingly.

Candy Crush Mania

Jaliyah, Aleksy, Imani, Jhené, Jamal, Trevor, Tavon, Shanique, Kleavon and I are best friends. I've known Jaliyah, Imani, Trevor and Jhené for 11 years; since I was 2 in nursery, and met the others in the first year of elementary school. Kleavon and Tavon are twins, both born on the 23rd of June.

"Hey, last one to the see-saw is a sloppy Joe!" Jhené squealed eagerly, and we all reacted fast, running stealthily to the park ahead.

Jamal and I reached the see-saw first, and we both cheered and jeered at the others for losing the race. Jamal tried to jump up onto one side of the see-saw while I attempted to clamber up slowly on the other side; failing miserably since our communication skills were weak!

THUMP! Onto the ground I fell, dust and mud ruining my uniform.

"I'm weak, how're you falling like that?" Aleksy laughed with everyone else then pulled me up from the ground.

"Oh thanks for having my back guys" I say sarcastically while rolling my eyes.

"You're welcome dearest Miracle" my friends said in creepy unison, and then we all burst into laughter, falling over onto the grass with tears dripping out of our eyes.

"Don't give me jokes" Imani hiccuped through her laughter, thrusting her box-braided filled hair up to the sky.

Shanique, Kleavon, Tavon, Imani and I get up first and start bidding our good byes to the rest of our squad.

"See you guys tomorrow!" We began to cross the road and all of a sudden, a speeding car appeared from the top of the road, flashed

Does Candy Crush Have Magical Powers?

a sinister beam of lights and before Imani, Tavon, Shanique and I could scream out "Wait!" or "Stop!" or "Watch out!", it was too late. Kleavon turned around in the middle of the road, barely able to see anything. Crash! The car knocked into him straight, and within a matter of seconds, he fell to the floor, unconscious, blood coming out of his head and scratches on his arms. Immediately, the others who had begun to walk home already ran towards us.

"Kleavon!" We screamed. Tavon started hyperventilating and made a move to run and smash the car of the person who knocked out his brother.

"Tavon, stop. It won't do any good; we need to get an ambulance A.S.A.P.!" I shouted whilst crying hysterically.

"Imani, you have a phone, use it, c'mon!" Shanique said.

Imani fumbled in her pockets, heaving and puffing, and eventually found it. Her fingers kept slipping as she was attempting to dial 999.

"Here, I'll do it," Trevor sniffed bravely. He took Imani's phone and dialled 999.

"999, what's your emergency?"

"My best friend just got hit and I don't know what to do and we need an ambulance and all of us are here on the curb waiting and it's so upsetting and we're scared that he's really hurt or something he's just lying there unconscious and bleeding and…and-"

"Calm down, it's alright. Can you please give me an address, street or area code?"

"You have a locator or something, don't you? Just be here soon!"

Candy Crush Mania

Trevor shouts back.

Slowly I crawled back over to Kleavon and tried to prop up his head slightly.

"Please be alive Kleavon." I whispered softly into his bruised ear.

The ambulance sirens began to sound in the distance and we waved it over to us, all huddled around Kleavon.

For the next 2 hours we all found our way to the hospital and waited anxiously for the results. It was now 8:37pm and all that we could smell was baby powder and sanitizer, making my stomach churn while I walked up and down the corridor.

"Shanique, do you think he's... dead?" I quivered anxiously as my brain rolled back and forth, burdened heavily.

"No. Don't think like that Mimi; let's not think negatively, Kleavon will be okay." Shanique replied.

Finally, a pretty, squinty-eyed nurse with soft brown eyes and naturally curly hair clattered down the hallway and came to us.

"Your friend... he's... he's..."

"He's dead isn't he?" Tavon whispered.

"No! Not at all, well... he's in a coma." The nurse said.

"A - A coma?" Aleksy mutters.

"Yes, umm... We've put him on life support. It was a pretty bad crash and he's going to have surgery immediately." The nurse replied.

Jaliyah, Aleksy, Imani, Jhené, Jamal, Trevor, Tavon, Shanique and I look nervously at one another. Jaliyah choked back tears and stared up at the bright lights dotted around the hospital

Does Candy Crush Have Magical Powers?

ceiling. I looked over and squeezed her hand.

"Everything will be okay in the end. God has a plan and no matter what we're all in this together. Right guys?" I said.

"Exactly. Don't let your negative thoughts dampen your mood. He'll pull through. Oh, and I forgot; the doctor said you can come and visit him anytime between 2pm and 9pm."

As Kleavon lay in this vegetative state for three whole months, I went to visit him faithfully every Friday after school and every Sunday after church. It was very frustrating for me because I could not bring him anything. Generally when you visit someone in a hospital you bring them flowers, fruit or chocolate (if they're allowed) but his case was different. He just lay there lifeless and it hurt my little heart to see him there like that. The doctors advised us to talk to him and touch him gently as he was aware of his surroundings even though he could not talk or emote. Hospitals are boring, so to while the time I would take my iPad with me and play different games; especially Candy Crush, which Kleavon also liked playing before on our revered 'Gadget Fridays' with Mrs Mathieu. He couldn't play along with me but I always kept the music on so the room was flooded with the candy Crush background music. After all didn't the doctor say we can chat and play with him and even sing his favourite songs as these will increase his chances of snapping out of the coma?

For 12 painful weeks I went without fail to visit my ailing friend. I missed his company and the whole class was like a graveyard

Candy Crush Mania

without Kleavon. Being a Christian establishment we never ceased to say prayers on behalf of him and his family. His Mum had to leave her job to nurse him daily, and even though I was still in many ways a child I wish I was God and had a magic wand I could wave, bring Kleavon out of his coma and wipe that perpetual look of despair on his mothers face.

When I started playing Candy Crush at his bed side, my mum thought I was just disturbing the peace but when the doctors assured her that it was perfectly fine to do so they allowed me to play on while she chatted away with Kleave's mum.

One Sunday after service where I had been singing the Movie version of "This little Light of Mine I'm Gonna Let It Shine", my Mum took me to the hospital. We bought some cakes and a few apples and drinks which we shared with Kleave's mum. As soon as they started chatting about fashion and recipes I just rolled my eyes, took out my iPad and positioned myself next to Keave's head and started crushing candy to the sound of the Candy Crush music.

" Tan Tan tan tan, tantan tan ...."

Then I got a colour bomb and the narrator said all the usual stuff he says when you are about to win a game but when he said "sugar crush" then "sweet, sweet, divine", I thought I saw Keavon twitch, and twitch again and then I thought I saw him open and clench his feeble fists which had been lying lifeless for three months. I shouted "mummy Keave just moved"!

Does Candy Crush Have Magical Powers?

Both of them jolted from their sits like rockets at take-off. His Mum started to cry and pressed the button to call for a nurse or doctor. They all rushed in and with closed eyes Kleavon stuttered;

"C...c-c-candy c-c-crush,"

His Mum asked, "What did he say?"

"C...c-c-candy c-c-crush," he repeated weakly as I bent down to listen.

He said "He wants to play Candy Crush I think".

"Miracle!" My mum shouted, "He only said two words!"

"Don't be a drama queen; make way for the doctors to do their job."

We all moved away amidst the commotion while the Doctor listened again and announced

"Madam he indeed said Candy Crush". The doctor further explained that one thing which usually helps get patients out of a coma is "fond memories". In the case of Candy Crush, he said that it was likely that because it was a game Keavon had played very often, it was stored in his brain. So when his friend Miracle kept playing it over and over again to him, it must have triggered sweet memories in him and a desire to play again.

This time around everybody was shouting, jumping, crying, hugging and doing all manner of things. I jumped and hugged Keaves mum as my Ipad fell and cracked but I could care less. My friend was back!

The doctors were all amazed.

"To think I went to medical school for 7 years and a 10 year old has helped heal her friend by playing Candy Crush!"

Candy Crush Mania

"I think I should download that game and declare Sundays a Candy Crush Day in this hospital!"
What's your name again little girl?" the doctor asked.
"Miracle," I said.
"Really?" he replied.
"Yes, Miracle Hurd is my full name."
"You are a miracle worker you know".
"Don't put that in her little head doc she can be really vain this one", my mum said hugging me fondly and ruffling my hair.
"I think you should take a job with the children's hospital and be our youngest ever doctor!"
Nothing can describe the euphoria that went on in the hospital that day. There were shouts, hugs, tears, screaming, jumping and dancing all at once. That day marked the beginning of Kleav's slow but steady race back into good health.
I left the hospital that Sunday on cloud nine, not knowing exactly if what I had witnessed that day was a dream or reality.
When my mum and I went home and told my dad, he thought we telling tales but he soon realised that we were not joking at all. Until now, his iPhone was the only device in our house on which Candy Crush was never downloaded. That blessed Sunday he downloaded the game unto his "Holy Land", of a phone saying:
"If this game also has miracle healing powers, I don't want to be the only one to lose out"
We had made another Candy Crush disciple to add to our list of converts and enthusiasts. That Sunday afternoon went like a mirage and I couldn't wait to get to school on Monday and tell

Does Candy Crush Have Magical Powers?

everyone what had happened in the hospital on Sunday. On Monday morning I was the first to get up, bathe and get dressed for school. Usually I'm the one who lazes about; dragging myself around and it usually takes a couple of shouts from my mum before I get myself ready for school.

I was totally unprepared for what I met in school that morning. Outside our school was jammed with photographers, police vans, camera men and paparazzi amidst neatly dressed pupils all awaiting what I do not know. As my father spun his red Jaguar and stopped someone pointed at his car and my dad asked:

"What is going on in your school today?"

"I don't know", I replied

"Are you having a special event or something?

"Miss didn't tell us anything on Friday". I said.

But before I could open the door, cameras on long poles of all sizes and shapes rushed at me with a barrage of questions. Then someone just picked me up and all were chanting: "Miracle, Miracle, Miracle, Miracle, Miracle, Miracle", and boy was I glad that I had worn my black PE shorts under my skirt that morning. It suddenly occurred to me that I was not the one who would be the first to share the story about Keavon to my mates.

Someone in the hospital had leaked the information to the local newspaper and I had made headline news that morning. There was so much commotion my dad jumped out of his car in his usual protective manner to find out what was going on. He only had to take one guess as a fellow parent brandished the morning paper in his face. The police had to quickly intervene and I was carted

Candy Crush Mania

into the school like someone on the witness protection programme.

To be quite honest, I don't remember what we did at school that day; all was a haze. Throughout the six hours of school I felt I was either daydreaming or sleepwalking; not a moment felt real! Walking into each class of the day and at break and lunch, all I heard was the continuous cheers from everyone; teachers and students alike.

I went home that day and because I could not put in words my gratitude, I decided to write this poem. It was a thank you note of sorts to Candy Crush about the way I felt. I expressed my love for the game. I was overwhelmed by the happenings of the weekend and the start of the school week. That night I could not sleep I stayed up till 3am and just began to write this poem.

Candy Crush

I'm crushing candies till 3am,
Swiping sweets, sugar mayhem,
The colour bomb is a beautiful thing;
Chocolate ball with sugary things.
Use all the boosters; then I just pay,
Look up the time; full lives all day.

I'm on Level 50; Odus unlocked,
Lollipop Hammers I'm 'boutta concoct.
Extra time plus extra moves,
Bubble-gum troll eats all the bad food.
Candy Crush Saga is my Kryptonite,

I promise to expedite my full lives,

Does Candy Crush Have Magical Powers?

I've been looking at the board for too damn long,
Mouth is drooling while listening to the CCS song.
Soon enough I'm gonna need some candy,
Some sweets or bon-bons will come in handy.

Kleav is back and my life is sweet.

Chapter 4: Playing With My Younger Brother

"Love is a force more formidable than any other. It is invisible - it cannot be seen or measured, yet it is powerful enough to transform you in a moment, and offer you more joy than any material possession could".

Barbara de Angelis

After my mum gave birth to me she waited seven years before my brother Excellence was born. In a way I can say that we are worlds apart, in the sense that when it comes to gaming we have very different tastes.

It's cold almost half of the year and even in summer most of our life is spent indoors. My mum often rallies us up for long walks in the evening to keep fit and most Saturdays we go swimming as a family, and I'll sometimes go to the gym instead. I always look forward to these times in the pool, as it is a time for me to bond with my brother. I love horse riding too but the last time we booked Excellence for a riding lesson he cried and refused to mount the horse. Even though he keeps expressing a desire to ride with me, he is just not ready yet. So that leaves very few things left for us to

Playing With My Younger Brother

do together.

Our Saturdays in the pool is without doubt a very pleasant experience but when we come home, it is usually confrontational as we struggle to find movies and games which we both like. To be honest, I don't mind watching Doc McStuffins, Jake and The Neverland Pirates or even Disney Pixar's Cars with my brother; but not for hours on end and day after day. Excy has a very interesting way of watching TV; anything he likes or any episode that makes him laugh causes him to pick up the remote, rewind it, laugh again, rewind it, and laugh even more, then again and again and again giggling excitedly. It's funny I must say, but after a while it becomes tiresome and simply annoying.

So I was over the moon when my dad bought me my first iPad, since I no longer had to spend gruelling moments in front of the TV watching Jake and the Neverland Pirates.

I would rather be in bed watching continuous episodes or movies on Netflix, or chatting with my friends online. But when I started playing Candy Crush, my inquisitive little explorer of a brother asked me to show him how to play it. He is quite quick at learning anything, and as a result within ten minutes he had figured what the game was all about and was now trading his revered remote control for my iPad.

Believe me, he is a real charmer my brother. When I refuse to give him my iPad he goes and tells mum first.

"Mummy, Mimi is not sharing her iPad with me".

Candy Crush Mania

"Ask her nicely," my mum would say. "It's because you did not ask nicely."

"Mimi you are very pretty, can I have the iPad please"

I, like all girls like a compliment and each time I look at his cute little face I am unable to say "no" to him. Although sometimes I would rather have had the iPad all to myself, I am happy that we at least have a game we can play and interact together.

Mum and dad are always complaining that I should play more often with Excy. They always say children play with children, adults play with adults.

"A child's first play mate is their sibling if they have one," my parents always say. Therefore, I had to try my best to be a big sister to Excellence. I don't do too badly (if I do say so myself) but I must say he is an interesting character. Sometimes he behaves like the king of a country which I honestly do not know of.

Excy can be very independent when he chooses to be. He can play all by himself and manage the computer and the iPad without any input from anyone else and basically minds his own business. But sometimes he wants so much attention I wonder if he was born to be a king in a land far, far away (as said in Shrek) and landed in our house.

Imagine that Excy has got two hands, two legs, two eyes and everything else yet he wants me to hold the iPad while he plays. And when I complain, mummy will just look at us and giggle. He

Playing With My Younger Brother

will be watching TV, eating a snack and I would have to hold the iPad while he swipes frantically on Candy Crush.

Not only do I have to watch Disney Pixar Cars, Lightning McQueen and all the shows he likes, he thinks I am his unpaid personal butler. As if that is not enough; even after daddy bought his own iPad he still wants to play with mine too!

I used to be furious but mummy explained to me that "Excy is only little, we should all indulge him till he is a little older."

She explained to me what the role of a big sister is; to care for, comfort, play with and protect their younger sibling. She said I should try and create beautiful memories of my childhood with my brother so that when we grow up we will still be fond of each other.

Playing Candy Crush with my brother helped build a bond between us and as we played and giggled, my mum began to thrown a stealthy look over at us once too often and I knew it would only be a matter of time before she became a disciple of the beautiful game.

Chapter 5: Mummy Joins The Game

"Sometimes I think that the one thing I love most about being an adult is the right to buy candy whenever and wherever I want".

Ryan Gosling

One blessed day my sister-in-law who lives in Dubai with her husband Ulrich and their two beautiful kids Kaleb and Kayla called me and said they wanted to come over to England and spend their summer holidays with us. We were overjoyed because we have prayed for the family to catch up on stolen time and let the next generation of kids get to know and bond with each other.

I was excited but soon switched to panic mode as I wondered what I would do with four children under the same roof for four whole weeks. My challenge was how I would find enough activities for them to do to keep them busy, entertained and happy. Now, many of you can say

"How hard can that be"?

"It's just a bunch of kids, surely an adult will find enough things to

Mummy Joins The Game

do with them".

In our case there would be three adults in the house which is not a bad ratio. That is one-is-to-one point three three three... Given that in most developed countries the ratio of adults to children in a childcare situation is one adult to 5 children; our situation was going to be pretty decent. If you think that would calm me down it did not.

I knew my own children and I was already having a tough time settling first TV misunderstandings, iPad disputes and now Candy Crush fights between them but for some reason I thought it would be a cool idea if I actually tried playing the game with them. In so doing I would find out what it is that they love so much about this game and then when their cousins came for holidays they would have something to share with them.

Apart from that I come from a different generation and our growing up experiences are miles apart from that of our children. Now in our days (that makes me sound pretty ancient) you didn't have to worry about what game children played or what to do with them during holidays. In the 1970's in my home country there were no TV's let alone computers in individual households. Very few children had toys or electronic gadgets to play with. You were lucky if you got a ball. Most of the time when you needed a toy as a child you made one. If you needed a ball you bundled some old newspapers wrapped them in polythene bags and rubber and *voila.* When children needed a car they would ingenuously use disposed milk tins and other housewold waste items to build a car

Candy Crush Mania

which they enjoyed just as much as the models in our western shops. There is a specie of grass we call the *Bahama Grass* which has many tiny roots as fine as hair. We would simply pull it out wash the soil off and there was our very own own Barbie ready to play with. We would sew dresses for her and braid her air. We did not have everything but we had something and we had a blissfull childhood full of sunshine. We never lacked playmates as all neighbourhood children came out to play in the sun and only went in to eat, have a wash or go to sleep.

Times have changed and we as parents have to face the challenges head-on. Adults play with adults and children play with other children. But the difference is miles apart as these high tech generation of children are always bored especially because they don't get to go out as much during the cold winter months. All they do is snuggle on the sofa and watch TV or play computer mames such as Lego, Batman, Movie Star Planet, and play pssssssssssst "Candy Crush".

"Don't say I told you".

As I played Candy Crush Saga, the game began to grow on me as it does with many other people that play the game. I found myself playing everywhere; during break time at work, on the bus. Even during school runs as I waited for the children's school gates to be opened, I would lean on the school gate and crush away. But I realised I was not the only one playing Candy Crush. Many of the mums stood there with their mobile devices and when you spied, they were all crushing candy, some with muted sound and some

Mummy Joins The Game

could care less if the music was reaching other ears. It seems there is a revolution brewing a new generation of gamers spearheaded by women. Candy Crush is a very social game. "Do you play Candy Crush?", has become a popular conversation opener between some women I have met.

I write poetry as a hobby in my spare time and one night after the kids had gone to bed and relaxed on the sofa to endulge in my guilty pleasure. After several successful rounds of Candy Crush, I found a poem forming in my head and I rushed to my kitchen computer and just wrote the words down as they came to me.

I remember sitting down to plan the holidays with Gordon and the first thing he proposed was the fact that we needed to buy a third iPad if we wanted some peace and tranquillity during the summer holidays. He expressed in no uncertain terms that he would not like to have to settle disputes between the children. So I suggested that before going out to buy another iPad he should first call his sister in Dubai and find out if the kids have an iPad already. Fortunately they both had an iPad to themselves.

My task was getting tougher I had to sit down and do some planning. I planned indoor and outdoor activities like bowling trips, horse riding trips, swimming trips, days out and of course an introduction to Candy Crush. But the catch was that apart from an occasional touch and go, I had never really been a Candy Crush fan. I did not understand why the whole world was going crazy about a "children"'s game like that.

Candy Crush Mania

At this point I had no choice anyway. I had four children looking up to me to give them a memorable summer holiday, so my journey with Candy Crush began. If playing Candy Crush was one of the ways I could keep them happy I was willing to give the game a try. Little did I know that I was getting into a labyrinth and would soon be arguing with the children over a silly game!

Chapter 6: Candy Crush Follows Me Everywhere

"The great thing about candy is that it can't be spoiled by the adult world. Candy is innocent. And all Halloween candy pales next to candy corn, if only because candy corn used to appear, like the Great Pumpkin, solely on Halloween".

Rosecrans Baldwin

If you want to know anything about computers or online games just ask my daughter Miracle and you are sure she will find an answer to your query. Sometimes when Gordon teaches me something on the computer and I don't get it I just call Miracle later for a refresher course and ask her to walk me through it.

And she usually succeeds 99% of the time in teaching me many things I have failed to learn before. One day as she was trying to show me something and clicking away without even letting me touch the mouse I told her:

"Miracle please can you talk to me and let me do it myself following your instructions? Instead of just doing it! It means next

Candy Crush Mania

time I will still have to call you to help out".

She replied and said to me "Mummy you know many times I don't even know the answer but I know that by trying I will be sure to find a solution". Like father like daughter!

Wow! I learnt a thing or two that day. I learnt to be daring and to troubleshoot, something Gordon has been urging me to do for many years. Whenever I encounter a problem I just throw in the towel or yell out for help.

There is no quick fix to anything and you've got to navigate your way into and around problems. This is one lesson we have all learnt as we played candy crush. You are given five lives and so many moves at the beginning of the game. It is now up to you to find strategies to achieve the set target within the limits given to you. Off we went to Candy Land.

So here I am again taking lessons on Candy Crush. It did not take me long to figure the game out and start enjoying it. Maybe even more than the kids.

Candy Crush is like candy. Everybody enjoys it. Boys, girls, men women, the young and the old, we have all at one point stuck that sweet lollipop into our mouths, closed our eyes and allowed it to transport us to a land of phantasmal sweetness. Hmmmm hmmm we all groan with pure delight as we devour some of the most tasteful things ever made with sugar. Candy Crush has grown on me like candy or chocolate grows on adults.

Candy Crush Follows Me Everywhere

I play Candy Crush everywhere: in the kitchen, bathroom, living room, on the bus, on school runs, in the park, while I am waiting at the doctors surgery, on train journeys and anywhere where I can hold a phone or iPad. I absolutely love the game and although my initial reason for learning to play was to be able to interact with the kids and have something in common with them, my enthusiasm for the game went past parenting. I am now a celebrated candy swiper and can be seen hopping from device to device playing manically and licking my lips as if eating real life candy.

I write poetry as a hobby in my spare time and one night after the kids had gone to bed I relaxed on the sofa to endulge in my guilty pleasure. After several successful rounds of Candy Crush, I found a poem forming in my head and I rushed to my kitchen computer and just wrote the words down as the came to me.

Candy Crush Bonanza

Candy, candy candy everywhere
Red, yellow, blue, purple, orange can't decide
Left, right, centre candy makes me stare
A veritable feast my eyes cant' deride

I taste and close my longing eyes!
I crush and crush and crush!
I savor and whisper as time flies
Candy Crush what a rush!

I swipe up, down, left, right and centre
Then I see the cookie splash away
Excited like little kids that banter
I know this game has come to stay

Candy Crush Mania

Chunky chocolate cookie full of sprinkles
Red, yellow, blue and purple flavors
Candy colors and patterns twinkle
Hmmmm I close my eyes and savor

Then I open my eyes and I swipe
Booom! The candy bomb explodes
Boom boom as more candy I wipe
Candies falling like rocks on slopes.

I hear his deep voice bellowing
That makes my blood rush.
An angelic sweet sound following
Then an emphatic Sugar Crush

I listen and savor the minefield
Of various sugar coated candies
A Kaleidoscope of colour like a field
Blooming with all colors of lilies.

A conclusive bellow divine!
I thought it was over but not yet
Boom! Boom! the sugar blows my mind
Fireworks in this minefield is what you get

So much sugar so much candy
This should be outlawed
As staying up all night like a dandy
Cannot give you pleasure without flaw

Down and down they tumble
Crushing each other as they roll
Sweet sweet sweet the candies rumble
Candy in all its colour as a fop that strolls

Hmmmm tasty I am like a kid
In a candy store and am loving it.
Like a child with box and no lid
Then his voice makes my heat to skid

Candy Crush Follows Me Everywhere

Crush, crush, sugar crushing
Red, blue, orange, green purple, green
Hmmmm, hmmm Divine as candies dashing
Then his voice hits me like light on a screen

And my heart skips a bit as I stir
Sugar crush as his voice pops
And I jolt bolt upright so I can stare
Like curious kids in candy shops!

I am in Candy lover and will not grovel
Am crushing virtual candy day and night
Hurray! I am on my way to the next level
Even if I stay awake till the morning light.

Brenda Hurd: Written 4am

Chapter 7: Battle Over The Cookie

"Peanut Butter M&Ms in the fridge, I always have a giant bag. Every cookie and candy I put in the fridge, it always manages to taste better when it's cold".

Hilary Rhoda

Excellence calls the colour bomb "the Cookie" as it reminds him of one of his favourite snacks; chocolate cookies with maltesers. Because he loves the colour bomb so much, we decided that being the baby of the house we would allow him to swipe our color bomb each time we get one and he was near. He loves this arrangement which once broken brings him to tears and only his dad can calm him down.

In fact, one day we were playing together and a cookie appeared but I was so excited that I immediately swiped the color bomb. He was so mad at me.

"Mummy you ruined my day" he screamed.

"I am not playing with you anymore"

"You ruined my life"

His piercing words carried on since he was so upset.

Oh Lord help me! Excy takes this game seriously and for him it is a bitter tragedy to not let him swipe special candy. Then I started

Candy Crush Mania

begging him:

"Sorry Excy you can swipe the next one": but Excy wasn't having it.

"No I'm not playing anymore"

Getting ready for "water works", I started to prepare for the excuse I would give my husband this time as to why "his son" was crying.

"Waah, waaah, waah, waah"

"Daddy, mummy swiped the cookie"

"She's not my friend anymore"

"Brenda, Brenda what have you done to my son?"

"Why can't he ever play with you guys without crying?"

"Do you hear him crying when I play with him?"

"And what is the cookie anyway?"

Sheepishly I approach Gordon's study and explained what the cookie is and why Excy is crying. Excy jumps into Gordon's arms and they match into the living room where Miracle is busy swiping away on her own iPad and Gordon proclaims:

"As the head of this house, I declare that from today henceforth, the cookie belongs to Excellence. Anyone playing Candy Crush under my roof should give my son Excellence Hurd the right to swipe the cookie or this game will be banned in this house."

"Excy, give Daddy a high five"

They high five each other and Gordon takes him for an appeasement trip to the supermarket to buy cookies. Mimi and I can barely contain the laughter by now and we sheepishly promise to do as we've been instructed as we collapse on the floor in stiches.

Battle Over The Cookie

"Daddy speaks like David Cameron in Parliament or President Obama passing a new health bill," Mimi chuckles.

We carry on laughing, hands in the air in solemn promise as Excy retorts:

"This is not a laughing show"

"Don't mind the silly girls, let's go to the supermarket and daddy will buy you something nice".

Gordon takes the cue and, shaking his head, whisks Excy away before another confrontation brews right before his eyes. They both drive off and Mimi and I are left laughing on the floor like two wild cats. At least we can have a few more rounds to play in peace. But from that day forward "The Cookie", sure did belong to Excellence as of the presidential decree made by his Excellency Gordon Hurd President of The Hurd Colony and writer of its uncoded constitution.

There are two worlds in Candy Crush: the real world and the Dream World with an owl called Odus. While playing one has to keep a balance and make sure that Odus does not fall as that would signify an immediate end to the game. This game has gained worldwide popularity and the fact that developers are still working day and night to create new levels for our enjoyment, means that the it has come to stay. A book has a beginning and an end but Candy Crush is an open game, an unfinished pilgrims' journey and its players won't rest until they have conquered the temptations that lie ahead.

We were all enjoying the game and our anticipation grew as the days drew near for our summer holiday visitors from Dubai.

Chapter 8: We Are Candy Crush Lovers

"Juice has staying power. It's not a fad. Once people have tasted POM Wonderful, they say they are addicted - and it's a good addiction to have".

Lynda Resnick

Though having multiple iPads had solved some of the disputes with the children, the Candy Crush tree had now grown a new branch in the person of mummy herself. Although I had downloaded Candy Crush onto my phone, I would occasionally sneak away Miracle's iPad when she was not watching and disappear with it either into the toilet, bath or kitchen.

This usually happens when I have lost all lives on my game but still wish to continue playing, I would look for the next available device and pinch it when they are not watching. But I'd rather take Miracle's iPad as we can always sort it out amongst ourselves. If I dare take Excy's iPad, he will not only cry the house down but use his usual statements on me.

"Daddy's my friend".

"Daddy! Mummy took my iPad off me".

"I am telling Daddy of you Mummy".

We Are Candy Crush Lovers

Fancy a grown woman like me being told off for "stealing" a child's toy? Not funny at all right?

On this blessed day I had lost all lives on the Candy Crush game on my phone and I looked and saw that Miracle was distracted on the phone as she was on Skype with two of her best friends Imani and Shanique. Well, you know young people with earphones plugged in, arms flailing in the air, laughter and giggles: the third world war could break out and they won't hear. I quietly snatched the iPad and made my way to the bathroom.

My privacy was short lived. I hear a knock on the bathroom door and said "Mummy is in here", I was secretly hoping she would say: "Bye see you later."

But no, Mimi was after her iPad. Skype conversation over, she was sure to go back to Candy Crush.

Shame on me; she found me frantically swiping candy and asked: "Mummy can I play Candy Crush with you?"

I thought in my head 'Mimi would never have come in here even for a thousand bucks!' Hmmm what Candy Crush can do.

"Yes" I said. "If you don't mind".

She did not even answer, she just sat on the bath tub which is is pretty close to the toilet seat and we continued playing Candy Crush like it was the most natural thing to do. We played and played and lost. Swiping candy left, right, up and down giggling and emoting like two children. Taking turns and helping each other we took out time to enjoy each other's company. The fact that I was answering the call of nature in the process was not an issue.

Candy Crush Mania

That's when Miracle burst out laughing hysterically like she does sometimes and tears were rolling down her eyes. I wondered what she was laughing about but could not help joining in the laughter. We laughed and laughed till our sides hurt then I asked Miracle:
"What are we laughing about?"
"Mummy look at us".
"You on the potty"
"Me on the bath and we are playing Candy Crush"
"Mummy seriously I think we are addicted to this game"
We resumed the laughter and continued the game and won that level.
"Yessssssss! Yesssssss! Yesssssss"! we both shouted.
Then we stood up for the Candy Crush Victory Dance which involves swaying our arms in circular movements shaking our booty and waist in good measure. Then Gordon called.
"What is that commotion about?"
"Nothing" we replied and sheepishly exited the bathroom like two kids who had been caught stealing candy from a shop. I guess that is when the first seeds of the idea to write a book about our experiences were sown. From that time we no longer made a secret of our love for the game.
We were all enjoying the game and our anticipation grew as we looked forward to welcoming our august guests into our house for the summer holidays.

Chapter 9: Candy Crush Summer Holidays

"The bond that links your true family is not one of blood, but of respect and joy in each other's life."

Richard Bach

The countdown had started and daily the kids will look at the kitchen calender and ask how many more days till their cousins visit. Excy in his own manner will ask:

" Mummy how many more sleeps till Kaleb and Kayla are here?"

"Six more sleeps," I would reply.

The same question the next day and the next and the next till finally he asked again.

"Mummy how many more sleeps till Anty Sylvine, Kaleb and Kayla are here?

"One more sleep finally" I tell my eager little boy.

That night he was so excited he could not fall asleep. He usually needs only two games of Candy Crush to fall asleep, but that night we must have played over ten games before he finally slumped and slept. I crept out of bed and joined Gordon to clear space in his study which is also our guest room. We made the bed up and retired for the night as Gordon would be taking the long drive to Manchester Airport to pick up his sister and her kids. Our car can only take 5 passengers so the boys had to go to avoid the tears of Master Excellence from flooding our humble home. He was over the moon as he high fived his dad. They both dressed in an identical three piece suit as some diplomatic convoy going to pick up the President.

Miracle and I stayed at home to finish preparing lunch and relax before pure summer bliss hit our home. Though Miracle confessed she was rather nervous because she was afraid she wont know just what to say or do with them, I assured her she just had to be nice, be herself and not struggle to put up a front as things would take a natural turn.

We were so anxious we kept staring out of the window each time we heard the sound of a car engine. Finally we were so excited we just left and stood in the front garden to wait, unable to contain our excitement anymore. Finally our red Jaguar with its distinctive sports engine, roared and we roared long with it skipping and screaming like teenagers on a college road trip.

We were shouting so much our neighbours came out to look and find out what was going on as we are usually a very quiet and unobtrusive family, very polite and always minding our own business. Gordon was just laughing as we could barely wait for the car to come to a stop. As Sylvine emerged from the car we

Candy Crush Summer Holidays

jumped into each other's arms in a bear hug. The kids were all staring at us amidst tears, laughter and mumblings which we both cannot remember as we swayed from side to side. Now guys in this family we are expressive! We do hugs and kisses and victory dances and all so watch out. I remember when my husband published his first book, I hugged the UPS van driver who delivered the parcel and the guy was wondering what the feistiness was all about. He wondered if he was carrying a long awaited heart for a transplant or something but that's just us.

I opened the back door of the car and lifted Kayla into the air, the poor girl was just smiling and must have wondered why aunty was so overjoyed. I ruffled Kaleb's air and hugged him as well but he had grown a little much to be picked up. Being a boy I also wondered if he won't tell me like Excellence does sometimes that he's not a baby anymore. The last time I saw Kaleb was in Germany when he was barely one week old but now he was all grown up and would soon turn ten.

Gordon had to remind us that we needed to go in and there were suitcases that needed to get into the house. Now Sylvine is a veritable shopper I expected 3 suitcases between them but they had 8 full suitcases, and they had barely been able to fit them all into the car. Some had to be slipped under their feet and they rode with feet suspended in the air like astronauts on a virgin voyage.
"Man oh man Sylvine what do you have inside them", I queried.
"It's only three weeks holidays you know. Unless you have done a

runner on your husband and did not inform us"

"No Ma B", she replied as she fondly calls me. "It is our stuff and presents."

We half dragged half carried fully loaded boxes into the house and upstairs to their room. We were all flabbergasted at the extent to which she had gone to buy presents for us and the kids. It can only be likened to a wardrobe overhaul. It looks like she bought presents for every birthday and Christmas she had missed in all our lives. We were moved and very grateful.

Lunch was served and I had prepared a special meal which Sylvine asked for. She loved the food so much that she ate it twice every day for 4 days. They were all knackered from the flight, the change in time zones and the frenzy that travelling usually brings with it, so they retired early.

They were up early the next day as they normally are in school at 7am in Dubai and I was surprised to see them already playing in the back garden.

"My! Good morning I thought you guys will still be sleeping! What are you doing up so early?". I asked

"Good morning, we are still adjusting to the time. Anyway we normally wake up this early so its not a problem."

The day went speedily as we prepared lunch for the kids especially as Sylvine had already declared what she would be eating for the next few days. After lunch Gordon retired for his usual afternoon nap and we all sat in the living room to wind down.

The children were already trying to get to know each other but I

Candy Crush Summer Holidays

landed my usual question as a bonafide Candy Crush Ambassador.

"Kaleb and Kayla do you play Candy Crush?"

"No we don't" they replied

"What about you Sylvine?"

" I always get countless requests on Facebook but I have never tried it."

"Can I teach you how to play Candy Crush?"

"Yes", they all replied

I could see the glint in Miracle's eye as she finally had something she could do with her cousins. They all rushed upstairs and brought their devices and so began their own Candy Crush journey. Sylvine downloaded and added the Candy Crush app unto her phone and started playing along as well.

We had made three more converts for our Candy Crush Clan and we were overjoyed. The kids all loved the game and would sit in the living room to watch TV and swipe candy. Kayla was intrigued at how much we loved the game.

"Anty Brenda is this your family game?" she would ask.

"Yes," I replied.

"But why does Excellence play on every body's iPad when he has his own?"

"Don't worry Kayla he is the baby of the house. Don't mind him. We just indulge him otherwise he'll start crying and tell of us."

The holidays were going just great and I was really happy that the kids were enjoying themselves. One day we went bowling and it was so much fun. Excellence loves bowling even though he can hardly carry a bowling ball. The bowling company provides a sliding slope for its younger users but trust Excy he refused to use it.

"I am a big boy, I can do it", he said.

When he tried to make his first throw we were all in stiches as both boy and bowling ball went down and we had to rescue him.

He stood up dusted himself and pointed to us laughing.

"This is not a laughing show"!

We knew better to stop our laugher or take it somewhere else. Gordon patiently showed him how to use the slide and he used it from then on. Although Sylvine was bowling for the first time she beat us all at the game and we all started hailing her like her students fondly call her: "Mama Africa Power, Mama Africa Power, Mama Africa Power"!

It was a really pleasant time and the kids would gladly have stayed in the bowling alley all day and night but there is an end to every good thing.

Next day we all woke up early as it was Friday and we were preparing a surprise birthday party for Kaleb. Sylvianne and I kept disappearing to the shops buying things and hiding them in the storage closet or in the back garden till the coast was clear to bring inside. Now Sylvianne is an avid shopper so these trips to the supermarkets and shops just provided her the thrill she gets dress shopping. Well for your information only Sylvine can come on a 3 week holiday with 8 full suitcases. She also left with 8 full suitcases. Hmmm we told her you would be lucky if your baggage is checked in! Anything she found in the UK that was not in Dubai

Candy Crush Summer Holidays

she bought!

Saturday was Kaleb's 10th birthday and as the doorbell rang at 9am I knew it was the bouncy castle company. I rushed to the door and let them in through the back garden, where they set up the bouncy castle. You know the engine that blows air into the castle is very loud and once the castle was fully blown the kids looked to see what was making so much noise behind the house. When they saw a full sized bouncy castle in their very own backyard they flew downstairs pyjamas and all and plunged unto the bouncy castle. That's it the party had already begun. Though other guests were due to arrive at 2pm for them the party had already begun. We all came out and wished Kaleb happy birthday as the kids bounced up and down on the castle. I looked at them rather enviously and Gordon eyed me and said:

"Brenda please don't get on that bouncy castle its for children only!"

Ok I had been challenged here was I minding my business and not intending to bounce on the castle and Gordon is insinuating that I want to play. I eyed Sylvine and she eyed me back and in one swoop we both took a dive unto the bouncy castle to satisfy our inner child. Gordon just shook his head:

"Women never grow up; and especially my wife! I don't trust her around children. If they are playing candy Crush she plays, if they are moulding play dough she does it as well, if they are picking worms...."

" Ewe yukky": the children all shouted.

Candy Crush Mania

"Don't worry Brenda I will one day build a school for you and you can have all the kids, bouncy castles, swings and games you want. And I'll make sure to sew your own uniform because I know you won't mind wearing one at all". Gordon laughed and shook his head as he sauntered off leaving us to our childish games.
Laughter for good measure and our curiosity satisfied, we left the children to play while we cooked and decorated the house.

When the guests started arriving the kids were still on the castle in their pyjamas and we had to pry them off *manu-militari* to have a bath and dress up. It was a beautiful day and Kaleb the Birthday boy was very pleased. It is amazing how children so easily flow together with no gimmicks and lengthy introductions. All the kids that came that day had never met Kaleb before but that did not stop them having a fantastic time. Except for a few tears and and one or two accidents on the bouncy castle with Kaleb, the party was a resounding success and Kaleb was very grateful.

When the bouncy Castle company came to take the castle at 7pm the kids still wanted to play. The guys suggested that for an additional 20 pounds they would leave the castle till 9am the next day. As Gordon went upstairs to bring some money the skies proverbially opened and a sudden gush of rain descended and we just decided to pass. The kids were now soaked and we needed to dry them up and change them into fresh warm clothes.

That night the kids all slept like logs of wood. In fact they did not

Candy Crush Summer Holidays

even need their usual bedtime story and candy crush game. I am always a happy mum when kids go to bed without a fuss and I can retire early.

Next day we all took it easy. There was enough leftover food to feed us for two more days so I did not have to cook. After lunch we retired to the living room as it was pouring outside and there was no hope of any outdoor activity. We sat down to watch a movie and soon got back to our favourite hobby. Candy Crush!

Now Candy Crush is a simple game but don't let its simplicity fool you. Some levels of the game are pretty tough especially the levels with chocolate that keeps creepily growing back if not crushed. Now as a family our toughest game was level 70.

> "Level 70 is another very tough jelly level. The combination of many blockers and teleports makes it challenging for even very experienced candy crushers. This board requires re-rolling for strong opening matches on the right side. Horizontal striped candies and combos made on the left can help you break jellies on the right. The chocolate needs to be cleared in the first several moves for the best chance to win." (http://bit.ly/HardestLevelsAtCandyCrushMania).

People this level was a real challenge for us! We played and played and played and kept loosing. Even after buying lives we still could not win. We played it for 2 months and no win was in sight so we decided that we would exercise patience and restraint, desist from buying any lives and try to win by our own boot straps. After all that is what playing is all about. On that same Sunday we finally cracked level 70.

Candy Crush Mania

I was sitting on the couch and almost at the same time that I got the colour bomb that brought us victory, Kayla got a colour bomb on her game as well. As she bent down to show me saying,

"Aunty Brenda I got a Cookie yeah"

"Well done," I said not knowing that Excellence had seen both colour bombs and was looking forward to swiping them. We simultaneously swiped the cookies and I called out to Mimi to announce we had won level 70. We all jumped up and started our victory dance

"Oh yeah oh yeah, We won we won we won,"

In the midst of all that jubilation, we heared

"Waah, waaah, waah, waaah" and when I turned to look it was Excellence.

"Kayla why did you swipe the cookie?" Excellence admonished.

"Waah waah waah, I will tell my daddy of you"

Kayla looked bewildered as she did not know what she had done. She had committed a mortal sin. In our house the colour bomb belongs to Excellence as per a presidential decree issued by Gordon. If anyone gets a cookie only Excellence is allowed to swipe it.

"Kayla why did you swipe the cookie? The cookie belongs to me".

Kayla looked even more bewildered

"But Excellence this is my iPad!" Kayla said.

"Waaah waah waah", the crying continued.

"But the cookie belongs to me!" Excellence retorted

Waah waaah waaah…..Excellence upped the decibel of his crying

Knock knock on the door as Gordon entered.

Candy Crush Summer Holidays

"What is going on here.? What is this brouhaha all about and why is Excellence crying again?"

Mimi and I stopped dead in our victory dance. We had continued celebrating while all this was going on.

"Daddy daddy Kayla swiped the cookie. Kayla is not my cousin anymore. Waah waah waaah."

"That does not change anything", Kayla said. "Don't be annoying".

"Ok Excy calm down daddy is here now and will get to the bottom of the matter."

Mimi and I were so ashamed of ourselves me especially to think that I was dancing while Excy was crying. I sheepishly stopped the gyration and sat down. Gordon took one look at me then Mimi then asked what we were dancing about. So we explained that we had won level 70 which had held us captive for 2 months and Kayla had swiped her own cookie on her own iPad although Excy was hoping to do so.

"Excellence", Gordon said. "The fact that your cousin did not give you her cookie does not mean than she is no longer your cousin" You have to learn that everyone also likes the cookie. So if you smile and hug Kayla I will take you out to Macdonalds."

"I love you Kayla". Hug hug.

Kayla looked even more bewildred.

Gordon calmly explained to both kids that it was just a game and they should not let that get between them.

Kaleb was in stiches laughing his eyes out.

"I've never heard anyone say "I will tell my daddy of you" so many times in one day."

Candy Crush Mania

In his usual style Gordon picked up his car keys and carted the children all to MacDonalds for a make up meal.

We were glad they were out. Mimi passed on McDonald's and remained with us at home to continue crushing candy and finish the victory dance.

Now kids are very mischievous when they came back we continued our chill out day. I had lost all lives and was waiting for a recharge when I fell asleep. I woke up suddenly to lots of laughter and giggling. I knew the kids were up to something! Miracle and Kaleb had made a video of me snoring on the couch with the caption "mum falls asleep while waiting for Candy Crush lives to refill. Her snores can scare the tooth fairy or Mr Yeti". They were threatening to put it up on YouTube and Instagram to get views.

" I swear this will go viral," Kaleb said.

Hmmm hmm I cleared my throat "No one is putting that on any social media! Give it to me."

They giggled and ran out of the house.

"Promise to take us horse riding and I will delete the video," Mimi said.

"I promise," I said lifting my hands up to heaven.

And so went our summer holidays and we could hardly believe that 3 weeks had gone by so soon. Their departure day was like a funeral as no one was left dry eyed.

Chapter 10: Candy Crush Ambassadors

"Happiness quite unshared can scarcely be called happiness; it has no taste."

Charlotte Brontë

As our love for Candy Crush grew we were not ashamed to share in with our friends on Facebook or in real life. Somehow we had inadvertently become "Candy Crush Ambassadors" in our circle of friends. Whenever our family, friends or kids friends came to visit the first question was.

"Do you play Candy Crush"?

"What level are you at?

If they were not Candy Crush enthusiasts, you can bet your bottom dollar that by the time they left our house they would be converted and would go home and start their own crushing battles. Most times when we had guests with children Gordon will excuse himself upstairs because if he stayed any longer the conversation always turned to Candy Crush and he would see a bunch of children swiping candy in all directions and on all manner

Candy Crush Ambassadors

of devices. At the end he would barely have space to sit down as kids would be swapping devices left and right showing off their jokers or progress made in the game. When he found himself perching precariously at the edge of the couch like a bird on a dying tree branch he knew it was time to go.

If our visitors were already playing Candy Crush, we were excited to know what level they were at. Unbeknown to us we had in our journey become Candy Crush gurus. If they were stuck at any level in Candy Crush we would take upon ourselves the challenge of playing and winning that level and putting a smile on their faces as well as teaching them the Candy Crush Victory Dance.

Gordon always wondered what a grown woman was doing with a bunch of children screaming their heads out, laughing, smiling, and dancing. In the beginning all he knew was whenever there are visitors there would be commotion down stairs. Initially he thought it was just children and their usual rough play until he would come down to get some tea, a pot of yoghurt or mangoes, his favourite, peep through the living room door and see a bunch of kids and in the middle of them a full grown woman, his yours truly wife gyrating to some so-called victory dance. He would shake his head and wonder what his wife was turning to.

Excellence would look up see his dad at the door and say:

"Dad come and play candy crush with me," and Gordon would reply:

Candy Crush Mania

"You have your mother for that. She has the patience to do that. Infact she has enough patience to play for both of us."

Mimi would giggle and say: "Daddy you don't know what you are missing.

"I pass on this one baby. Hang on to mummy don't worry when we get permission and land we will open a school and give mummy as a present. There she will have the space and enough children to share all this love and energy in her bones with". I would just laugh and continue swiping on whatever device was made available to me.

Gordon's Samsung Galaxy phone was the only device on which a Candy Crush App was never downloaded. But even that did not last forever. I was lucky to sometimes have my own phone. But many times I was just a supervisor and consultant, overseeing the children as they enjoyed the game.

"Please ! Please! Pretty please Daddy the children would all shout"

"Yes Uncle" The other children would echo as he is fondly referred to.

"Pretty pretty please".

"No thank you guys", he would say in his usual jovial manner.

"Just imagine a grown man like me playing Candy Crush! Soldiers are in Afghanistan fighting wars and I am playing? Naah"

Candy Crush Ambassadors

And off he would go mango and drink in hand to continue his own pursuits. We'll all laugh and continue our Candy Crush craze.

When the kids are stuck they would come to Miracle or me, the undeclared professors of Candy Crush though, to be quite honest, Miracle was the champion of us all with robotic fingers she could swipe a hundred times in a nano second.

While this would be going on they would still have their favourite TV programs going on and would still find time to watch, play, fight over the remote control and quarrel over whose turn it was to put their favourite movie or show. I was always the arbiter ready to settle any disputes and calm any crying child especially mine as he cried more than any other child.

Miracle found it very interesting when her friends were visiting and they'll always tell her:

"Your mum is so cool".

"Oh yes", she would tell them.

"Wait until you mess about then you will know that my mum is as strict as a headmistress".

"All the same she's proper cool".

"Just behave yourselves then and we'll only ever have to deal with Mummy Cool", Miracle would tell them.

"I heard that"! I would counter.

Candy Crush Mania

They would all shy into their little corners and get back to their game like nothing happened. Many of them left with joy on their faces and a spring in their steps as they were sure that if they had been stuck on a particular level once they set foot in our house we would crack it and send them back home with an onward journey in Candy Crush land.

I had become to them like a "Candy Crush Mummy" serving them tea, cakes and biscuits or whatever was available as they played their games. Sometimes when it got all heated up or we had to wait for lives to recharge, we would take a break and go into my kitchen which fortunately is large enough to accommodate a party of kids.

It was not uncommon to find me apron, hat and spatula in hand with 3, 5 and sometimes up to 10 kids splattered with flour, egg shells, butter and all as we tried to bake cakes and cookies. The kids would be screaming and enjoying every minute of the day and many of my friends wondered why the kids were always saying "we want to go to Aunty Brenda's house".

I chose to enjoy these experiences with them as I knew this would form part of their childhood memories. Unbeknown to us we were forming a bond which grew stronger and stronger each day by playing Candy Crush together.

Chapter 11: Family Bonding Through Candy Crush

"Brain scans show synchrony between the brains of mother and child; but what they can't show is the internal bond that belongs to neither alone, a fusion in which the self feels so permeable it doesn't matter whose body is whose".

Diane Ackerman

One of the things that parents complain about is that they are unable to connect with their children in a gadget oriented age where every form of entertainment is screen based. Some parents have given up trying and its not uncommon to go to a house with kids and stay for one hour without hearing the sound or voice of children playing. If you peep into the average household today you would see a bunch of kids stuck behind screens playing games and doing stuff online which their parents have no notion of. On the other hand children are also complaining that their parents take no interest in the things they do.

As a family, playing Candy Crush together has contributed

Candy Crush Mania

something and helped alleviate this problem for us. We realised that it is not only good for pedagogical reasons to be interested in what your children are doing online, but it can also be a fun experience. Today as parents we are not shy to try out the games they play even if we may not develop the same interest as we have done with Candy Crush. Our children know that they can play with us and be silly.

Through playing Candy Crush we have grown closer to our children and spend more time with them. I normally read with them in the evening after they do their homework and for a while I struggled because the baby of the house Excellence now wanted to play Candy Crush at bedtime. The way I grew up bedtime meant all devises off, all lights off and bed. Now Gordon is the kind of parent that is willing to try new things and be flexible with children. He always says that rather than having children upset make a compromise with them but make sure you have control. He said if playing Candy Crush would lull the kids to sleep, I should try it out as long as they don't see it as an excuse to stay up all night. So I decided to give it a try.

Being and inquisitive mum I looked online and realised that several parents use music, story book pre-readings and recitals to put their kids to bed. In the case of one mum her child can't fall asleep without her in the room so she sits patiently at his bedside and plays Candy Crush with the music on till he falls asleep.

Now I realised I was not an alien mother and my son was not just being unreasonable. Now it takes one to two games for my son to fall asleep. He loves the Candy Crush background music and it seems many people even adults seem to love the music, especially the Candy Crush soda music which King spared no expenses to create. While researching this book I found out that the theme music to Candy Crush Soda Saga was recorded by The London Symphony Orchestra, home of Europe's finest musicians.

Why is Candy Crush So Amazing?

Oscar Wilde once that said the only way to get rid of temptation is to yield to it. However, it appears that if one succumbs to the temptation of Candy Crush, one just can't stop.

It is just amazing how many things you can do and say with children when you bring yourself down to their level. There are many lessons that we have learnt from playing Candy Crush. There has been a lot of media frenzy about the nature of Candy Crush but the very things for which Candy Crush is criticised are the virtues we have found in the game.

Candy Crush Awakens Your Inner Child

Sweets, cakes, chocolates, ice-cream! Anywhere in the world these are a child's favourite. And many of us adults always reward children with candy. Do well in school and your parents promise you ice-cream. Do your chores and grandma presses a pound or two in your hands and the first thing any child thinks of buying with their pocket money, is candy. Even as adults candy and chocolate

Candy Crush Mania

is our secret pleasure at home, work or school. It is no doubt that the game Candy Crush resonates with so many people of so many different ages. The good thing about Candy Crush is that it does not land us on a dentist's chair yet gives our eyes an optical and emotional feast. Palm says:

> "Many people have had a very positive feeling about candy since they were kids... it makes for a really nice visual game board with a lot of color and interesting shapes. In fact, when you play you feel as if you're transported into an entire Candy Land experience. The game pieces are candy, and the homepage for the game looks like the traditional Candy Land board, with your Facebook friends' pictures displayed as pieces on that board, sitting at whatever level they're stuck on. (http://bit.ly/BBCAtCandyCrushMania).

Candy Crush Tends to Teach Goal Setting

One of the most important lessons in life is learning how to set and achieve goals. Goal setting is a forgotten art which needs to be relearnt if we must succeed in most things we do. Gordon says in his book *Christian Prosperity Secrets*:

> "A goal is a well thought out, clearly written plan of anything you want to be, do or have. If anything is important to you, it warrants a goal. Some call it an objective, target or plan. Whatever you call it, it deserves your time and attention." (Gordon Hurd:2013,P.64)

The way Candy Crush functions is that it sets a goal that is to be achieved with a certain amount of moves. Let us take level 33 of the game as an example. In level 33 the objective is to clear all jelly in 14 moves. The goal is to clear all the jelly and the tools you have to do so there are 14 moves only. It is now up to the player

Family Bonding Through Candy Crush

to find a strategy to clear the jelly with their limited supply of 14 moves. The more striped and special candy you make the easier it will be to win the game. Otherwise the player has to buy more moves to complete the game or ask friends if they play on Facebook.

Each level contains a certain objective that must be completed in a given number of moves (or time frame); some levels require clearing "jelly" off the board by making matches on top of them, reaching a certain score, getting ingredient items to the bottom of the board, or having to clear certain amounts or combinations of candies. Levels may also contain blocks to make them more difficult, such as meringue or liquorice swirls, chocolate (which spreads across the board if left uncleared), bombs (which end the level if they are not matched before they go off), multi-layered icing blocks (with tin plates as the last layers), and others. Boosters can be earned or purchased to provide assistance during levels.

The game comes to an end not only when you reach a particular target score but either when you accomplish the target set out at the beginning of the game or when the player runs out of moves.

Candy Crush is Age and Gender Neutral

Although demographical research figures show that Candy Crush is typically played by women aged 25-45, wider research also confirms that it is played by people of all social strata.

Candy Crush Mania

Candy Crush is one of those gender-neutral games....Unlike so many online games, it doesn't involve killing, fighting, strong male characters or highly sexualized female characters." (http://bit.ly/WomenAtCandyCrushMania).

Personally, and I am sure many women agree with me, some online games are very violent, contain strong language, a lot of swearing and adult topics which people especially women and children, do not necessarily want to encounter in a game. When I play a game I want to relax and enjoy myself. Some may have fun shooting down enemies but I would rather crush candy. A nice game of Candy Crush is my reward at the end of a hard day of work.

Some of the online games are games mostly men would enjoy. All the shooting, fighting and gesticulation. Worse of all is the noise produced by some of these games. If earphones are not used and you stand at the door of a teenage boys room, you would think that a veritable third world war was going on in there. Candy Crush offeres a pleasant, violence-free, age and gender neutral alternative to online games. This makes it a perfect game for all the family.

My son has in the past had nightmares after playing games with shooting involved. Now he enjoys one or two games of Candy Crush in bed and sleeps like an angel. With Candy Crush, men, women, young, old all play the game with varying degrees of intensity but above all is the language and music of the game that

Family Bonding Through Candy Crush

really appeals.

Taking a look at the state of video games as a whole, it's virtually impossible not to see Prof. Griffiths' point. The vast majority of games made since the 1980s either involve ultraviolent action or impossible standards of female sexuality, usually both. Those that avoid these unfortunate tropes are generally given little to no attention by the male-centric industry. One 23-year-old London resident told the Arab News that she enjoyed Candy Crush, but emphatically stated that she was "not a gamer." Candy Crush and similarly designed casual games may be a huge step toward the democratization of modern gaming.

Candy Crush is Pleasant and the Music is "Divine"

Apart from the fact that Candy Crush is devoid of the themes of war, fighting, combat and swearing common in many online games, the game is played with very beautiful background music. What I find most soothing is the dramatic voice of the Candy Crush "narrator".

It also doesn't hurt that the game's visuals and soundtrack are exceptionally soothing, inducing happiness and relaxation all by themselves.

This tune follows the same melody line as the original Level Select, however, the change of instruments and the removal of the strong rhythmic line give this piece a dreamy quality. The main tune is being played by some sort of synthesised piano sound which has been modified to give it a softer feel. A glockenspiel plays in the background, its light, metallic notes producing a descending scale to provide the chords for the piece. A wind section is heard accompanying the background of this piece with single sustained notes, the group together creating sustained block chords to match the broken chords made by the glockenspiel. In the second repetition of the musical phrase, a flute is heard playing a harmony over the main section. I love this peice of music.

You would also see a score progress bar. Every time you crush candies (as discussed below), you earn points. These points will help you progress through the levels. If you do not earn enough points over the course of completing a level, you lose a life. Lose all five lives and you'll be forced to either wait until your lives refill or buy lives. Lives can be viewed on the larger game screen, where your progress through the levels is shown.

Candy Crush is A Social Game

When you leave school, your life moves in different directions and before long you have lost contact with all your friends. The invention of Facebook as a social media platform has transformed the way reunions occur. Games like Candy Crush Saga, Farm Heroes and Pet Rescue Saga go on to reinforce socialisation. It is amazing how you are playing Candy Crush and at the end it tells you which of your friends you have beaten and on what level they are.

Family Bonding Through Candy Crush

Social games - any game that allows you to connect with your friends through a social-media platform such as Facebook - have taken off. Whether it's Words With Friends, Kingdoms of Camelot or Candy Crush, the ability to play with, or compete against, friends is irresistible. Young says: "Look, nobody's coming to me because they have a clinical addiction to Candy Crush. It's more of a social addiction, if you will."

While writing this book I was actively playing daily on Facebook and I was amazed at the different people who were playing the game: men, women, teachers, doctors, engineers and pharmacists. So contrary to what many people may think it is not only "lazy women" who have nothing to do and sit on the sofa all day swiping candy and burning the kids dinners. This is stereotypical portrayal of the lovers of this game. My friend Marissa is a pharmacist and has a long three hour commute daily to London and back. She says that Candy Crush helped make the journey bearable and exciting for her.

In my experience Candy Crush seems to be a major conversation opener these days. We were on our way to a wedding last Saturday in a taxi and my daughter started to play Candy Crush at the back of the taxi. Immediately the driver heard the music he jumped from his grumpy self to life.

"Oh my God Candy Crush you too play that game? Am on level 450."

"Yes we do and we really enjoy it"

Candy Crush Mania

"But my Missus will throw me out if I continue playin".

We burst out laughing.

"I thought only women and children play Candy Crush"

" No!" he countered. "Why should women always have all the good things? Beautiful hair, beautiful bodies, more choice of clothes, make-up etc etc……a mans life is boring you know let us have some fun too that does not include guns."

And he is very right. We have declared Fridays in our home family, movie and gaming night. On Fridays because the kids don't go to school the next day, they are allowed to stay up longer and we as parents lay down all our extra work to spend time with our children. This was Gordons idea as we noticed a trend in the house. The fact that there is a computer in almost every room in the house meant that the children would eat and disappear to play on their own. We felt a kind of family loneliness and even though we were all living under the same roof we were having less and less quality time together.

On Gordons birthday last year Miracle forgot to buy a present for her dad, so she organised a movie night. She went on the computer and designed invites for everyone. She baked a cake all by herself and invited the family for snacks, movies and pop corn. Gordon still says that it is the best birthday he has ever had and the most ingenious idea for an 11 year old. Since then he proposed that we repeat that experience and declared Friday as a

Family Bonding Through Candy Crush

family fun night.

We can do anything on that night as long as we are all doing it together, be it watching a movie, playing Candy Crush or other games that allow us to commune with each other. You will be amazed at what kids can tell you when they are in play mode!!!!!. You kind of descend into their world and they find it easier to interact with you. Things they would otherwise not be able to muster the courage to tell you or ask you just seem to come up. This gives us an insight into their world and we begin to understand and appreciate the issues they are dealing with at school with their work or peer pressure and so on. Now we understand them more than we used to and our family bond has grown stronger than ever.

Candy Crush is a Media Sensation and Very Popular

Candy Crush was declared game of the year 2013 only one year after it was launched. Usually it is games and things around men and children that impress the world so fast. I attribute the high success of the game to its gender and age neutrality. King Digital Entertainment Plc has succeeded in creating a genderless, culture universal game with world wide appeal. According to Wikipedia:

> "Candy Crush Saga had over ten million downloads in December 2012 alone. In July 2013, it was estimated that Candy Crush Saga at the time had about 6.7 million active users and earned revenue of $633,000 per day in the US section of the iOS App Store alone. In November 2013, the game had been installed 500 million times across Facebook and iOS and Android devices. According to Business Insider, Candy Crush Saga was

Candy Crush Mania

the most downloaded iOS app for 2013 (http://bit.ly/PopularityAtCandyCrushMania).

Candy Crush has taken over whole nations like Hong Kong where it is reported that one in every 7 citizens plays the game. The game is also featured in Psy's music video "Gentleman". It is the 23 most downloaded game in Japan and the number one most downloaded game on the Apple Store.

According to review aggregating website Metacritic, the game received an average review score of 79/100, indicating generally positive reviews. Ellie Gibson of Eurogamer referred to Candy Crush Saga as 2013's "Game of the Year".

Candy Crush Tends To Teach Patience

The media has focused so much on the negative stories behind the gamer's experience that most people have failed to see some of the intrinsic good things about the game.

Each Candy Crush game has been designed to last about 3-5 minutes. If you are given 5 lives at the start of each game it means you have approximately 25 minutes to play. Well if that is all you play in a day whether child or adult, this cannot make you an addict.

Once your 5 lives are finished you are faced with your first lesson in patience! Now do you patiently wait it out, send a message to your friends on Facebook and wait till they send you lives or do you take out your credit card and buy lives and keep buying? Only you can answer that question.

Family Bonding Through Candy Crush

For us as a family we use the waiting time to chat, bond, share our experience of the game, go to the kitchen, wash dishes, bake a cake or do anthing worthwhile to while away the time. After one financial mishap by our youngest my kids have learnt to be patient, avoid wasting the familys resouces and know that they can't get whatever they want whenever they want to. We have a family budget and we often jokingly call Gordon the Chancellor of the Exchequer as he manges the family budget the same way he runs his businesses. "Waste not want not", he always reminds us.

Candy Crush is as popular as it is controversial and in the next chapter, we open the floor for varying opinions about the game.

Chapter 12: Candy Crush Diaries: Varying Opinions

"Different people have different opinions, and it's okay to respect all of them".

Juan Pablo Galavis

Unbeknown to many, Candy Crush has a worldwide family of players, fans, supporters, and enthusiasts. The head of this new global family is King itself which, like a father, caters to the needs of the whole family by constantly providing new episodes of the game for its offspring to enjoy.

There are so many online fora on which Candy Crush enthusiasts meet and encourage each other. Big brother to little brother, big sister to kid sister all are offering support, praise, encouragement and tips to each other on how best to play the game.

Candy Crush is a global phenomen in the field of online entertainment and I doff my hat to the developpers of this game

Candy Crush Diaries: Varying Opinions

who are working relentlessly to develop new episodes. The purpose of this chapter is to collate information gathered from some online platforms to give a snapshot of what people are saying and doing about Candy Crush.

bmorri03 Nadia • 3 months ago
This site has helped me many times. A lot of it is just plain luck. I like how this site explains what is going to happen at each level. I tried this site several times without getting rid of the chocolates and never could get a high enough score. Getting rid of them first is tough but keep trying. Eventually you will take them all of the board. Just as a reminder, don't accept any of your friends offers of lives until you have depleted your five that are there when you start. You can grab those later (look at the envelope in the upper right hand corner) when you have used up your five tries. Again it is just luck!

Mario Fanthom two months ago
Level 500 is insane!!! I think its as bad as, if not worse than 197!! Really tempted to boycott the game for a few weeks, but I am sooo close to finishing the entire game!

Gigi Marie Lexi Mee • 9 months ago
I couldn't remember 500 either so went back & looked at it. I only got 1 star so must've been hard! Lol.

satya Gigi Marie • 3 months ago
Who is the bustard founder of candy crush game?

Candy Crush Mania

Tygros Lexi Mee • 9 months ago

Agree, but wait until you get to 578. You can't beat it without buying add-ons. Malicious - easy month+

Gigi Marie Tygros • 9 months ago

No, that's not true that you can't pass it w/out buying boosters. You might be referring to the old version of it, where apparently you did have to have jelly fish boosters to beat it but they "nerfed it"(I learned what that meant reading about this level lol) so that now you don't need them. This level is really tricky....at first I was playing on my phone and wasn't even coming close to beating it. I honestly thought I'd be on it for ages. Then I played it on my PC and literally passed on my first try. Only one star but I could care less, I was just so happy to have passed it. I'd suggest to anyone having trouble w/ this level to play it on your PC vs phone. I passed w/ no boosters. I actually found 585 to be more difficult for some reason! But I think I'm in the minority w/ that one. 181 remains the hardest for me, it's the one I was on the longest. ugh.

Patty Penland Gigi Marie • 4 months ago

Level 437 is HARD.....ridiculous! I guess I'm done with Candy Crush...played this level well over 200 times and I rarely even get close!! Yes I'm in for some competition and enjoy a certain level of difficulty BUT what feels like impossible is Boring! Goodbye Candy Crush ....was fun while it lasted but guess this game is just too tough for me!

Minesh Patel Patty Penland • 2 months ago

Wait till you reach 789, most insane level I have come across, you can have stretgy for defusing 8 bombs which appears on opening

Candy Crush Diaries: Varying Opinions

of board, beyond that you just keep your finger crossed so that more green candies fall from top to complete order of collecting 77 green candies.

Television88 Patty Penland • 2 months ago

man...I read these comments here and have been stuck on level 40 for a while. are you people in the mensa branch of a prison so you have all day to figure this out.
Starting at 35, I started feeling the need of a 12 step program. Plus I have been doing Lumosity for a couple of years and I have been laying off it

Minesh Patel Television88 • 16 days ago

Nope we are normal people leaving normal life, just got retired from active duty on 1st Sept 14, started playing CC around on the 10th Sept, as off today completed 860 levels, without spending single farthing. Looking back I find 147, 181, 453, 461, 677, 789 & 829 most difficult levels, it will be wrong on my part to say that I cleared those levels, but real fact is, CC allowed me to clear mentioned levels.

Angelika Rose Gigi Marie • 8 days ago

For me 350 was the hardest. Took me three weeks top get passed it. Was about to boycott entire game when all of a sudden I achieved goal.

JannalSOP Tygros • 13 days ago

Candy Crush Mania

Not true, I haven't spent a single money on this game and so far im up to level 695.

Plantagernit JannalSOP • 12 days ago

I've not spent a single cent either (and *won't*) Just passed level 601.

Chris Mcleod Lexi Mee • 4 months ago

I got to 500 totally expecting to b stuck for some time as I remember some of these comments. Got lucky and completed on first try while watching some football. Buddy thought I was commenting on the football game when I completed the level lol

Lars Landover Lexi Mee • 3 months ago

I JUST beat 500!!! You can do it! Get those striped-wrapped combos, Lexi, and you'll be there. Good luck!

Athar Saleem • 10 months ago

Level 425 in real world and 250 in Dream world are the toughest levels of all 590 + 260 levels so far

jahstoney • a year ago

Level 84 of the owl levels is messing with me, and still Waiting for a ticket for 381. I refuse to buy anything.

Jahni Ballard Delatorre jahstoney • 10 months ago

I cant pass 84 of the owl for the life of me and I am a master at Candy Crush.

Gigi Marie jahstoney • 9 months ago

Interesting, I went back to 84 in the dreamworld to see what you guys were talking about. I passed it w/ 2 stars and was #2 in the top 3 of my fb friends but honestly don't remember it. Sometimes I find the dreamworld more difficult in general though than the "real

Candy Crush Diaries: Varying Opinions

world".

Raquel Dietrich Gigi Marie • a month ago
Level 84 of the dreamworld was pretty easy for me, got three stars on my first pass through.I had a much harder time with 128...still passed it though. Am on level 156 dreamworld now and 387 normal. Not been playing too much lately so my progress has slowed ;)

Brenda Joyce Cann • 9 months ago
Level 323 is killing me. Stuck for 3 weeks!!!!!!!!!!

Brenda Joyce Cann • 5 months ago
Omg this was awful, pretty much down to luck. Just make striped wherever you can and try to like them up all at once :(

Nova • 10 months ago
Why do you have a game that is impossible. Is it just for me because I refuse to spend any money? Level 165 hardly ever allows me more than 7 moves because of the bombs. If I am ever able to use all my moves the most blues I can get is 40-50 because there are not any on the board. I am taking a vacation from you. I don't need the frustration

Kimberly Torch • 6 months ago
The most difficult level for me was level 677....way too little moves to begin with and too many combos needed. All this with the added pleasure of constant bombs to tend to. I finally passed this devil level.. waiting at level 680 now for the next crazy episode to

Kimberly Torch Maria HD • 5 months ago
For both H Zammit and Maria... the only way that I was able to

pass it was save up my free hand switches and hammers and I bought extra moves BUT I only bought the extra moves when I got close enough; like 7 or 8 pairs of a possible good board and only needed 2 or 3 more pairs. You have to WAIT until you reach a board that feels right near the end... I never really buy extra moves but in this case, I was not letting the game go when I had gotten so close to the end, THEN I used my hand switches to make the extra pairs I needed to finish. Good Luck... the next episode is normal again :-)

ROLAND GALANIDO • 3 months ago

I am now @ Level 741, but i can only play on PC, not in my mobile phone & tablet. This starts when i completed level 725, everytime i ask the next level it only appears "To be continued... Soon there will be new places to explore, you may replay previous levels to gain higher scores and more stars"... Why? How many episodes/levels here in candy crush?

Maureen Lewis • 6 months ago

I am struggling with level 470. Any help?

Tygros • 9 months ago

Agree on needing to add in 578 - by far the most difficult. Incredibly so

daniel • 9 months ago

Level 578 was the hardest by far. Took me about a month..

A game can be picked up and continued whenever a player has a few minutes to spare – on the commute, in a lunch break, during a boring meeting or just before sleeping, in place of pillow talk. It is also social. A big part of the appeal is being able to compare your

Candy Crush Diaries: Varying Opinions

score with friends online. (http://www.theguardian.com/technology/2014/may/11/candy-crush-saga-games).

Negative comments

So many friends are wasting loot of time who is the bustard founder of candy crush

Daniel H • 4 months ago

Level 147 was designed by satan himself

Daniel L. Motes • 4 months ago

Level 417 is hard as hell! I've been stuck on it close to a month now! Stupid bombs and tornadoes just ruins the level!

This game has a very wide appeal and people of all ages and professional status are playing it. The oldest Candy Crush player I found so far online is 74 years old and this is what he has to say:

> "I Play every night for an hour. I have done this for the past 2 years. I have not bought any boosters but do take advantage of the free ones. I am on level 565 and have been here for some time. But, Like all the others, this one too will be beaten. At the ripe old age of 74, I throughly enjoy playing.... Besides, I am certain the game is good for this old man's brain!".

Chapter 13: Candy Crush, Celebrities and the Media

According to analysts, the recent ad campaign makes Sweden-based King the first mobile game developer to run a solo effort in the U.S. to promote one of its games.
TV viewers aren't strangers to ads featuring mobile games. They've seen Angry Birds being flung through on the air, for instance. But those TV impressions occurred within commercials for Windows 8. Windows 8 featured Angry Birds Star Wars in its ads and Rovio let its fans know the game was available on the new operating system.
(http://bit.ly/AdvertiseAtCandyCrushMania)

How can anyone do anything else with this addiction? Trust us, we know. Before long, you'll end up losing sleep, skipping meals, and/or nagging friends for extra lives, tickets and/or new strategies to get through tricky levels.

But you're not alone. And there's no reason to feel embarassed. It

Candy Crush, Celebrities and the Media

happens to the best of us. In fact, when we scoured through Twitter to read through tweets with the phrase Candy Crush, we found out that some of our favorite celebrities such as Kim Kardashien struggle through candies, jellies and chocolates too.

What adds to the popularity of this game is the fact that politicians, famous people and celebrities also play the game according to data gleaned from Facebook, twitter and Instagram. Jill Sanders even quoted the British Prime minister David Cameron as one of its players. He said:

> With its twinkly lights, hypnotic music and comic sound effects, it has millions of people in its grip - and, like 2010's Angry Birds, which even numbered David Cameron among its fans, it has become an online sensation.
> http://bit.ly/MediaAtCandyCrushMania

I do not know how true these allegations are but the fact remains that a British Member of Parliament also made headlines not for his political expertise but for being caught playing! Yes, playing Candy Crush during parliamentary proceedings.

> "Parliamentary watchdog rules NO-ONE will be punished over leaked photo of MP playing Candy Crush during committee hearing. Tory Nigel Mills caught playing on tax-funded iPad in pensions meeting. So Parliamentary watchdog investigated - to find out who leaked photo. Mole hunt now called off and whistleblower will face no punishment. Mr Mills apologised but keeps his seat and position on DWP committee"
> (http://bit.ly/NigelMillsAtCandyCrushMania)

The Prime Minister's reaction and pardon for the whistle blower

Candy Crush Mania

and Nigel Mills is an example of the attitude we should have. We all in a way have our guilty pleasures if we care to acknowledge them. Many large stores sell both alcoholic and non-alcoholic drinks. The choice is ours if we choose vodka over orange juice or water. Almost every home in Britain today has a TV set but are we all addicted to the screen? The choice is ours if we want to to be couch potatoes and watch all day to the detriment of our kids, personal hygiene and worthwhile pursuits That is why all devices have an off and on button. You can turn the TV on and off as you choose.

"David Cameron - himself a self-confessed games addict - defended Mr Mills.

'I know him well, he fights very hard in his constituency for people in Derbyshire, he works very hard in Parliament,' the Prime Minister said.

'I'm sure he will be embarrassed and he will work even harder in the future.'

Mr Cameron previously admitted to being addicted to mobile games Fruit Ninja and Angry Birds.

Asked what level the PM had reached on Candy Crush, his spokesman said: 'On that line of questioning, game over."

(http://bit.ly/NigelMillsAtCandyCrushMania).

Chapter 14: Candy Crush: The Good, the Bad and the Ugly

"There is just no getting around that turning bad things into good things is up to you"

Deepak Chopra

Though Candy Crush has received world wide popularity, it also has many critics who have lambasted the game for its addictive nature. Many people feel that it is sly to make a game and provide free downloads just to later make money off the gamers through in-app purchases. One exasperated player queried:

> "How can anyone do anything else with this addiction?" Trust us, we know. Before long, you'll end up losing sleep, skipping meals, and/or nagging friends for extra lives, tickets and/or new strategies to get through tricky levels. But you're not alone. And there's no reason to feel embarassed. It happens to the best of us. In fact, when we scoured through Twitter to read through tweets with the phrase Candy Crush in them, we found out that some of our favorite personalities struggle through candies, jellies and chocolates too". (http://www.rappler.com/life-and-style/technology/136-viral/26018-candy-crush).

Candy Crush first caught our attention when our youngest son

Candy Crush: The Good, The Bad And The Ugly

who was 4 at the time accidentally spent 150 pounds on the game. Gordon looked up his PayPal account as he wanted to make an online purchase and discovered that a significant amount of money had been spent without his permission. It was a Saturday morning and he summoned the whole family to a meeting in his study. We all use all iPads so it was not an issue of pointing one person as the culprit as there were multiple buys. Now the kids know that their dad does not summon except there is a house parliamentary issue to be discussed (SOS).

Starting with me, then Miracle, Gordon sought to ascertain who had made those purchases. By the time he got to Excellence he was ready to pee on himself because he could see that his dad was incensed.

"Do you guys know what 150 pounds is in a family budget?"

"Daddy are you going to flog me"? Excellence asked tears in his eyes.

Gordon and I don't believe in corporal punishment and we have always told the kids that they can escape any punishment if they tell the truth.

Excellence admitted that he had bought gold bars. Gordon admonished him, then hugged him, wiped his tears and told him to promise he would never buy anything thing without adult permission. As many of you know most smart devices operate a cookie system where passwords are stored, so Excellence did not need to know our Paypal debit card password to make a purchase. So it was our fault really. So now after every purchase we reset the device to make sure no such accident ever repeats

Candy Crush Mania

itself.

Now I am the Mrs Scrouge in the house and I said they should never buy any game at all. They should play with what they have. If they loose lives on Candy Crush they should wait it out even if it is three days as is sometimes the case. But Gordon stepped in to differ:

> "I am sorry I don't agree with you. We are online marketers, and I believe if you sell online you should buy online too. From every indication you and the kids enjoy this game and in my opinion you can buy within reasonable boundaries. You should understand that in this world anything you get free someone else has already paid for. If King Digital has to provide these games for free, they have an office, they pay staff, programmers, developpers, gas, electric, water and web hosting fees amongst others. How do you think they fund those things? They are not running a charity to create free games and let their workers go without a salary."

I knew I had gotten him started and I could see the glint in Miracles eyes as she knows she can get almost anything from her dad. We all play games, tennis, poker, bowling, football and cricket and I challenge you to show me where to get all your sports tools for free. As Beyonce says, "If you love it, put a ring on it". We as a family say, "If you love it put a price on it". If you enjoy a game pay for it because that is the only way to keep the developers and King programmers in their jobs and help them to continue bringing new episodes for your enjoyment.

After my son inadvertently spent that 150 pounds, the event has never recurred. The kids know if they spend 67 pence to buy lives or 99p to unlock an episode they have to forgo something in return. They trade in their ice cream for a game and that is fine with us. As long as the purchases are within reason it is fine with

Candy Crush: The Good, The Bad And The Ugly

us and we have better oversight as we are aware of what is going on.

I have other friends who have played up to level 500 and have spent less that 10 pounds all together. Their purchases are usually made to unlock different levesl as you are sometimes required to wait 3 days to continue to the next episode. Another friend got to level 400 without a single purchase. The decision to buy or not to buy lies solely with the gamer.

An article by by Jill Sanders and featured in the Daily Mail suggested that millions of people are caught in the grip of Candy Crush. He further revealed that women aged between 25 and 55 are the demographic most loyal to it and blow £400,000 a day playing Candy Crush. He continues that the game has millions of people in its grip and women aged between 25 and 55 are the demographic most loyal to it. Jill quotes Lucy Berkley, 44, as calling Candy Crush 'crack candy' because she's so addicted. He says Jenni Weaver, 40, plays for eight hours a day while Steph Brophy, 37, says 'It's taking over my life'. (Jill Foster for the *Daily Mail:*

(http://bit.ly/MediaAtCandyCrushMania)

Now with all due respect to her research one should always take a second look at such figures. When aggregate scores are placed out there, they can be misinterpreted and an alarm can be set off that is not necessary. Many adult men of high standing enjoy other games and movies, such as Angry Birds, Star Wars and Doctor Who and spend large sums of money on memorabilia and fan articles. As far as we are concerned, spending money on a game or fan article is a free will choice which every individual has to

Candy Crush Mania

make for themselves.

Statistics show that 97.7% of people are playing the games for free and only 2.3% actually pay for games. And for those that pay they are spending roughly 23 pounds a month on in-app purchases. I am not a maths guru but this indicates that those that pay for the game spend less than a pound a day to play. For people who smoke a pack of cigarettes a day it is 3 times cheaper to play Candy Crush than to smoke. If you drink a bottle of beer every day for £1.20, you are spending a total of £45 a month. If you add a good bottle of fine wine for Sunday dinner at £10 multiplied by 4 Sundays that brings it to £85 a month. Nothing in life comes for free. Anything you enjoy for free in this world has been paid for by someone. Even charity is not free: charities exist because someone out there makes money and has asked themselves how they can give back. If you live in a safe house, can call the fire service free of charge when your chip pan catches fire, or ring an ambulance when you are sick, it is because the tax payer has contributed to that public purse which you are now dipping into. And if we are really honest we play more than we pay. So I believe we should handle media speculations with care.

My son has a toy car collection which is a hobby he shares with his dad. Now his playing Candy Crush and buying lives for 67pence is a much cheaper alternative. But according to my husband he can have both as long as it fits in the family budget which he manages with all the stringency he can muster. Our kids

Candy Crush: The Good, The Bad And The Ugly

have learnt opportunity cost; they know they can't have it all all the time. They have to make choices. If you spend 99 pence for your game today don't bother running after the ice-cream van when it passes by. Full stop! End of story! Teach a child simple rules, stick to your guns and before long they will fall in line

As for adults they should know better. It is true that Candy Crush brings out your inner child but with time every novelty wears off and we readjust to normal patterns. I bought my first computer during my second year in university. In those days the only games available on the computer were solitaire and a few minesweeping things which I can hardly remember. That night after my computer was installed I sat on the computer and played solitaire till 5am. With barely two hours of sleep that night, I was falling asleep during lectures and only a hand writing expert or God himself could decode the notes I had taken that day. Did I ever play solitaire again? Off course I did, but never till 5am. Proof is I graduated from university and had I not gotten my act together I probably won't be writing this book.

It is the same thing that happens when you buy a new dress or a new pair of shoes. You wear it until someone remarks that you wore the same dress at the last party then you shy off and rethink your choice of wardrobe the next time you are going to the a party. Last Christmas my 5 year old son got a Power Rangers Megaforce costume which he adores. Excellence wore that outfit for seven days on the trot. He woke up in the morning, had his bath, changed his underwear and wore his Power Rangers costume. When I tried to complain his dad said it's a phase it will pass. After 7 days it was not looking good so I put him in the bath tub sneaked out and put it in the washing machine. That is how we broke that pattern. Does he still like Power Rangers? Yes he does but he no longer needs to wear his costume daily. Infact when he picked up his parcel from under the Christmas tree and saw that it was a Power Rangers outfit, he immediately peeled off his three pice suit, threw it on the living room floor and scampered into his costume. Thank God we had already taken family pictures as the rest of the days features Excy stayed in costume mask and all. It's been three months now and he has worn it just once during that period. So the word "addiction" should be used advisedly.

As a pedagogist, one cannot also minimise the fact that addictions are real issues in today's society so it is up to each person to know when they have crossed the line between sanity and insanity, love for a game and addiction. Every individual must decide for themselves. If you are stealing money from vulnerable people in your care to pay for anything then seek medical help. If your kids are late for school every morning because you were playing Candy Crush all night and did not hear the alarm then you need to check your priorities and get your act together. Responsible gaming is the *modus operandi* here.

But I reiterate that in our experience of playing this game we found out that the choice to spend money on the game still lies with the

Candy Crush: The Good, The Bad And The Ugly

consumer. We can go whole weeks without buying especially when we are on a winning streak. Sometimes you come so close to winning it is a shame not to pay 67 pence and and finish the game. But it is important not to take the fun out of the game by constantly buying add-ons. By playing on you develop resilience and a fighting spirit which can be transposed to other areas of life.

Chapter 15: Look To The Future

"You can't connect the dots looking forward; you can only connect them looking backwards. So you have to trust that the dots will somehow connect in your future. You have to trust in something - your gut, destiny, life, karma, whatever. This approach has never let me down, and it has made all the difference in my life".

Steve Jobs

We know many people out there play Candy Crush: children, boys, girls, men and women and that they all enjoy the game. Many are wondering if there is something wrong with them because they love this game so much. We absolutely love the game and continue playing it as a family. Through this game we have fostered an uncommon bond that transcends the online platform into all other areas of our family life. Even Gordon who initially was not sure what this Candy Crush craze was all about joined us as we wrote this book.

Candy Crush is a great way to relax and fill in on times when waiting at bus tops, doctor's surgery, school pick ups, visits to the park and other times when we have to queue and we have time to spare. Many children complain that their parents don't spend time

Look To The Future

with them. Conversely, parents complain that children are always locked up on their own with their numerous devices. We have found a game which we can all play. We use this game as a bonding tool and it has worked for our family. Anyone can make something positive out of any situation. That is exactly what we have done with our love for this game.

Now we not only play Candy Crush, we play Candy Crush Soda Saga, Farm Heroes, Pet Rescue Saga and many other games by King. But so far our most enjoyable has been Candy Crush, followed by Candy Crush Soda Saga (the 3D version of the game), and farm heroes which we played up to level 500 till Excellence inadvertently deleted the app.

Excy is master of his iPad. Though he is only 6 years old as at the time of writing this book, he is so computer savvy he puts some 40 years olds to utter shame. If he is trying to download other games such as Minecraft or Angry Birds, he would delete Candy Crush and when it's bedtime he would start asking to play it again. Then we have to find yet another app to delete and create space.
Now the question to ask is this:
"Is Candy Crush the biggest game in town? Is it a revolution that has come to stay or is just another fad that will soon die and be remembered no more?"

King continues to add new episodes to add new episodes which keeps people interested in the game. Personally I think Candy

Candy Crush Mania

Crush is here to stay. It has captured the imagination of the entire public and will stay relevant for years to come. This is further helped by the game's creator, King, which is developing spin-offs of the game regularly, improving current versions and expanding its reach worldwide. I foresee the day when Candy Crush will go beyond the household name that it already is, to be the object of academic studies in universities and even global conventions where enthusiasts, meet regularly to enjoy, share experiences and celebrate Candy Crush Saga and other games by King.

Subject to endorsement by King, we are planning a huge Candy Crush convention and trade fair after the launch of our book. This would bring together the creators, gaming companies, fans, enthusiasts, children, families and even mental health professionals, for a fun-filled week to enjoy and discuss the issues around Candy Crush in particular and gaming in general. The Police could be invited to talk about responsible gaming and internet safety for youths. Business people could display all their merchandise and it could be a family fun week. If held annually it will not only help generate income, it will be fun as well.

If recent history is any indication, that may not be too hard. The game launched on mobile in November 2012. Six months later, it is the highest grossing iPhone game in 17 countries, the highest grossing iPad game in nine countries and the highest grossing Android game in 20 countries, according to app analytics

Look To The Future

company App Annie.

Contributing to the game's addictiveness is its Facebook integration. Candy Crush Saga is the most popular app on Facebook with more than 15 million daily active users, according social app analytics website AppData. Every time one of these 15 million plays the game, whether on their mobile device or directly through Facebook on their PC, their player's friends are reminded to start playing again or are enticed to try the game for the first time. (http://bit.ly/AdvertiseAtCandyCrushMania).

As at December 2012, exactly eight months after it was launched, Candy Crush Saga had 10 million downloads with an estimated 6.7 million active users. By November 2013 it had been downloaded 500 million times on Facebook, iOs and Android devices. According to business Insider, Candy Crush was the most downloaded app of 2013. Fact is that the game derived its popularity simply by the sheer pleasure people derived in playing the game. Its users are increasing daily and now that King Digital Entertainment had taken the bold step of making a solo TV commercial, the first of its kind, its users are set to increase. The question many people are asking is" when will this saga come to an end?" I say maybe never!

I have studied Riccardo Zacconi's route from Dating Agency Magnate to King Digital Entertainment and found that he is a relentless man who would go the extra mile to uphold this venture. If he did not give up when he was almost going bankrupt and lobbying for investors, he won't give up now that he is quoted on

Candy Crush Mania

the stock exchange and has investors and top programmers at his service. The sky is the new limit. Candy Crush has taken whole countries like Hong Kong with 6 out of every 7 people playing the game. With a net annual income of over 500 million dollars, there is no limit to the resources available to keep this vision alive. Now with memorabilia and official fan articles like socks, t-shirts and Easter eggs hitting the market, we are yet to see more of this phenomenon.

Zacconi has not come this far to let this dream die. He is a glaring example of how a man follows his dream till it becomes a reality. Today more people play King games each month than live in the US, and the company is currently in expansion mode. The company is taking over Facebook's recently vacated British headquarters in Covent Garden. But the free caffeine and makeovers are a far cry from the company's early days. Back in 2003, a year after launch, money had run out. Zacconi was living rent-free in a friend's spare room, working without a salary. It was just before Christmas and he was flying home to Italy later that day. He and his co-founder Toby Rowland, son of the late mining tycoon and Observer newspaper proprietor Tiny Rowland, were staring at the fax machine, willing it to come to life. Zacconi recounts his agony while waiting for investors to respond to his request.

> "We had a promise from one of our angels [early backers] to invest in the company, but the piece of paper was not signed. We wanted to make sure we could pay all our

Look To The Future

creditors, and to do that we would have had to shut down the company that day."

King Digital Entertainment has grown from a near broke company to an award winning enterprise.

They have won several awards including:

- Fastest-Growing UK Company - Media Momentum Digital Awards
- Best Social Game - Candy Crush Saga, International Mobile Gaming Awards 2013]
- Gold Stevie Award - Bubble Witch Saga, 9th Annual International Business Awards (2012)
- Favorite App - Candy Crush Saga, 2014 Kids' Choice Awards, lost to Despicable Me: Minion Rush. http://bit.ly/AwardsAtCandyCrushMania

King continues to make headlines and I am positive it will continue to do so for a very long time. With King now branching out into official merchandise and theme parks, the company will continue to stay relevant. I hope I get the opportunity to shake Zacconi's hand one day and tell him all I have learnt from his life and games and how it has changed my family life. Candy Crush is currently the top grossing app on the App store and Google play in the USA, Brazil, Philippines, Italy, Australia, Singapore, Mexico, Malaysia, Ireland and St. Nevis.

I played Candy Crush every single day as I wrote this book. Sometimes when I need to pause for air, I go to Facebook and play. By the time I play a couple games I usually have fresh inspiration. After all the book is about Candy Crush isn't it? Playing the game alongside researching and writing this story was a great experience for my whole family and for you too I hope.

About The Authors

Miracle was born in Chemnitz Germany in 2002 as the first daughter to Gordon and Brenda Hurd. She learnt German as her first language as German was the language of instruction in the nursery she had to attend while her mum went to university. She also learnt English which she spoke at home and in church with her family.

From an early age Miracle loved to read and write little poems and stories on different occasions such as Father's Day, Mother's Day and Easter or just for fun. She started writing her first novel at age 9. She is still working on it and one day we will see it in print.

When Miracle came over to Britain aged three, she quickly learnt English and within 3 months she forgot German. The reason being that as she learnt English she was constantly mixing up both languages so her parents decided that they should stop speaking German to her in order to help her learn English fast and be able to integrate into the school system. Miracle is now breaching this gap by learning French in school and picking up her German with the help of her mum at home.

Brenda Hurd was born and raised in Cameroon where she attended Our Lady of Lourdes Girls Secondary School. After her "A" Levels she moved to Nigeria to attend university. She later on moved to Germany were she studied German and English Linguistics and Cultural studies. graduating with an MA.

About The Authors

Brenda loves literature and has been writing poetry since she was 12 years old. She has won several prices for her inspirational poems and has had the privilege of presenting her poems at various events. The Liverpool Central Museum in Great Britain also displays some samples of Brenda's poems.

Brenda holds a Master's Degree in German and English Linguistics and Cultural studies. She is a conference speaker and linguist fluent in English, French and German. She is a preacher, marriage counsellor, motivational speaker, goal setting expert, pedagogist, entrepreneur, business adviser, wife and mother. Brenda loves to work with children and young people and welcomed the idea of co-authoring this book with Miracle as a mother-daughter experience encouraging each other to take their writing seriously.

Brenda is married to Gordon Hurd and they have 5 children: Innocent, Paul-Silas, Miracle, Allegra and Excellence.

Brenda and Miracle can be contacted by email at: authors@candycrushmania.co.uk

Bibliography

http://company.king.com/our-games/

http://www.brainyquote.com/search_results.html?q=candy+crush+saga+king&pg=2

Hurd, Gordon: *Christian Prosperity Secrets*. Dignity Publishing. 2015.

http://www.withoutthesarcasm.com/how-do-i-clear-candy-crush-saga-level-92/#

http://bit.ly/WomenAtCandyCrushMania

http://bit.ly/WomenAtCandyCrushMania

http://candycrush-cheats.com/level-139/

http://bit.ly/HardestLevelsAtCandyCrushMania

http://en.wikipedia.org/wiki/Candy_Crush_Saga

http://candycrush-cheats.com/candy-crush-top-10-hardest-levels/

http://business.time.com/2013/11/15/candy-crush-saga-the-science-behind-our-addiction/

http://www.bbc.co.uk/news/magazine-25334716

http://www.dailymail.co.uk/femail/article-2463636/How-women-blow-400-000-day-playing-Candy-Crush-addictive-online-game-ever.html

http://www.gamasutra.com/blogs/MarkGriffiths/20131029/203442/Bitter_sweet_A_brief_look_at_addiction_to_Candy_Crush.php

http://phys.org/news/2014-03-candy-sweetens-gaming-female-audience.html

Bibliography

http://www.rappler.com/life-and-style/technology/136-viral/26018-candy-crush

http://candy-crush-saga.wikia.com/wiki/World

http://candy-crush-saga.wikia.com/wiki/World

http://www.bbc.co.uk/news/magazine-25334716

http://www.dailymail.co.uk/news/article-2867272/Parliamentary-watchdog-rules-NO-ONE-punished-leaked-photo-MP-playing-Candy-Crush-committee-hearing.html

http://en.wikipedia.org/wiki/King_%28company%29

andy-crush-saga.wikia.com/wiki/Candies

http://bit.ly/PopularityAtCandyCrushMania

http://bit.ly/MediaAtCandyCrushMania

http://bit.ly/NigelMillsAtCandyCrushMania

http://bit.ly/ConsultancuAtCandyCrushMania

http://bit.ly/AdvertiseAtCandyCrushMania

http://tvtropes.org/pmwiki/pmwiki.php/ThatOneLevel/CandyCrushSaga

http://tvtropes.org/pmwiki/pmwiki.php/ThatOneLevel/CandyCrushSaga

http://bit.ly/UdateAtCandyCrushMania

http://bit.ly/OxfordAtCandyCrushMania

http://candy-crush-saga.wikia.com/wiki/Levels

http://bit.ly/OxfordAtCandyCrushMania

www.ingramcontent.com/pod-product-compliance
Ingram Content Group UK Ltd.
Pitfield, Milton Keynes, MK11 3LW, UK
UKHW022225230426
12048UKWH00016BA/1059